D0208008

DATE DUE

HAVENS

**Recent Titles in
Contemporary Psychology**

Resilience for Today: Gaining Strength from Adversity
Edith Henderson Grotberg, editor

The Destructive Power of Religion: Violence in Judaism, Christianity, and
Islam, Volumes I–IV
J. Harold Ellens, editor

Helping Children Cope with the Death of a Parent: A Guide for the First Year
Paddy Greenwall Lewis and Jessica G. Lippman

Martyrdom: The Psychology, Theology, and Politics of Self-Sacrifice
*Rona M. Fields, with Contributions for Cóilín Owens, Valérie Rosoux, Michael
Berenbaum, and Reuven Firestone*

Redressing the Emperor: Improving Our Children's Public Mental Health System
John S. Lyons

HAVENS

Stories of True Community Healing

Leonard Jason and Martin Perdoux

Foreword by Thomas Moore

Contemporary Psychology
Chris E. Stout, Series Editor

Westport, Connecticut
London

Library of Congress Cataloging-in-Publication Data

Jason, Leonard.
   Havens : stories of true community healing / Leonard Jason and Martin Perdoux.
      p. cm. — (Contemporary psychology, ISSN 1546–668X)
   Includes bibliographical references and index.
   ISBN 0–275–98320–X (alk. paper)
   1. Community mental health services—United States. 2. Healing—Social aspects. 3. Community psychology. I. Perdoux, Martin. II. Title. III. Contemporary psychology (Praeger Publishers)
RA790.55.J37 2004
362.2′2—dc22   2004004632

British Library Cataloguing in Publication Data is available.

Library of Congress Catalog Card Number: 2004004632
ISBN: 0–275–98320–X
ISSN: 1546–668X

First published in 2004

Praeger Publishers, 88 Post Road West, Westport, CT 06881
An imprint of Greenwood Publishing Group, Inc.
www.praeger.com

Printed in the United States of America

The paper used in this book complies with the Permanent Paper Standard issued by the National Information Standards Organization (Z39.48–1984).

10   9   8   7   6   5   4   3   2   1

CONTENTS

SERIES FOREWORD

As this new millennium dawns, humankind has evolved—some would argue has devolved—exhibiting new and old behaviors that fascinate, infuriate, delight, or fully perplex those of us seeking answers to the question, "Why?" In this series, experts from various disciplines peer through the lens of psychology telling us answers they see for questions of human behavior. Their topics may range from humanity's psychological ills—addictions, abuse, suicide, murder, and terrorism among them—to works focused on positive subjects including intelligence, creativity, athleticism, and resilience. Regardless of the topic, the goal of this series remains constant—to offer innovative ideas, provocative considerations, and useful beginnings to better understand human behavior.

FOREWORD

It should be no surprise that many men and women, especially the young, find it difficult to hold their lives together in a society that gives them little education in emotion and character, and then treats them punitively and harshly when they don't measure up. Apparently we don't understand a basic equation: You make a heartless society, and you get confused and sociopathic kids. We also forget that those are indeed our children who turn to drugs and alcohol in order to feel alive or to avoid life altogether. Their confusion is an expression of need, not an evil nature. In other words, the people who crowd our jails, hospitals, and halfway houses are expressing society's illness. They are our children and require our care. The punitive feelings that arise when we see people devastated in their confusion are most likely tied to our own inner conflicts and memories about childhood and growing up.

We have to understand that we are dealing with wounded souls, not twisted personalities. The disturbances lie deep and bleed over from personal lives to family backgrounds to society's failures. It takes extreme depth of perception to respond to these problems effectively, and the best forms of healing may be quite mysterious, sometimes having little apparent relationship to the problem.

A case in point is the home where the fortunate ones can be held and embraced while they go through the rites of passage they were not given at the appropriate times in their lives. A house is never just a physical shelter. It has meaning as an image and as an emotional and imaginal environment. Troubled young people are often disconnected from happy childhood memories that give others the security to make it in a challenging world. A house can recreate that imaginal space and allow new family dynamics to appear and reshape the person. People often talk about emotional security as though it were abstract, something you force into your being by sheer will. But security comes from outside as well: from a building that has some echoes of the deep emotional home we all need; from people who accept us even if we've made serious mistakes; and from a focus for our feelings and fantasies. The Greeks honored a warm goddess, Hestia, as the hearth and focus of family life. Most of us know how important the warmth of a home is, but we don't always understand that people in trouble need it even more than we do.

A rite of passage includes not only a close villagelike community of support, but also a painful realization that to get along in life you have to deal with misfortune and bad treatment. Beneath a great deal of sociopathic behavior lies a child with too innocent a view of life. Small, controlled challenges can, to an extent, supply the rites of passage needed for healing.

There is a big difference, however, between toughening the personality—the way they do it in the Marines—and strengthening the soul. Belligerence and violence are the opposite of strength of spirit: they appear when personal power collapses. Helping people discover responsibility, choice, and even desire is a way toward strengthening individuals and therefore society as a whole.

In this book you will find stories about love and about power. The two are rarely apart from each other, and it is important to remember that they reinforce one another. Here you will see concrete ways imaginative leaders help those in trouble find themselves rather than become dependent on institutions. It is a new and promising imagination of how social healing works: not by setting up more programs, but by treating people in trouble as human beings, with certain basic emotional and social needs.

Ultimately, we, as a people, will have to learn how to house, and not institutionalize, those among us who get confused and lost. Not only our bodies, but our souls, too, need shelter. Emotional security means a sheltered soul, one that is protected from the onslaughts of a tough, generally soulless society. The pioneers in this book are leading the way, exploring how to provide that shelter of the soul.

The need for home is a yearning of the soul. It never ends, and it is the foundation of all secure actions. In this book you will read many stories of people going through life without an anchor and in search of home. You will learn about various ways hardworking people create homes and do their best to nurture the soul without any sentimentality or romanticism. You may glimpse pieces of yourself here, both as helper and the one in need. That's good, because, if you want to help solve the problems of our society, you will have to deal with yourself at every turn as you try to reach out to others. You have to be in touch with both your own need for security and your ability to help others find their deepest security.

It may be an obvious fact, but it's one not acted on nearly enough: we human beings need each other. We all get into trouble to some degree, and we all need friendship, expert counsel, and a source of security. Knowing the two sides of this basic human phenomenon, we can reach out to others in our common humanity. This book teaches how to reimagine this whole process, and now, in an increasingly technical and lonely world, we need this precious wisdom more than ever.

Thomas Moore

PREFACE

When is the last time you heard on the news about a heroin addict who had finally kicked the habit, gotten a job, and started to pay his rent regularly? Not likely. News like this is not sexy enough, and the recovering heroin addict is all too happy to disappear into the conformity of gainful employment. Good news doesn't usually make headlines; you will hear more often about things that go wrong.

Nevertheless, thanks to a refreshingly simple initiative, thousands of addicts did find that they could maintain sobriety at a much higher rate than in previous treatment attempts. And there is more good news. Thanks to similar solutions, debilitating, chronic medical illnesses can be managed with more stability than modern medicine can offer; persons who suffer from mental illness can be hospitalized much less often; and old age no longer has to be a time of isolation. To obtain these promising results, people are not removed from their lives to be placed in specialized professional settings. Instead, they continue to live in society at large, but within a small, protective community of their peers, with little or no supervision from authority figures.

We went to visit several of these communities, conscious of the delicate ethics involved in observing such a phenomenon. The people who inhabited these havens were in need of healing, and we were asking to be let inside their unconventional homes and intimate lives. Even with good references, it was a lot to ask; nevertheless, we were warmly invited in. The more time we spent in their company, the more we were rewarded with meaningful biographical material. In order to preserve confidentiality, we changed all the names. As we sat listening to their stories, time took a buoyant quality, and we felt a sense of camaraderie. That sensation is really what this book is about—the heartwarming experience of community people feel when they get together on a regular basis to talk about their history and day-to-day affairs.

The success of grassroots communities where residents find healing from seemingly hopeless cases of drug addiction, from chronic medical ailments, from mental illness, and from elderly hopelessness is well documented from years of research in community psychology (Jason, 1997), but academic publications rarely reach the general public (Bogat & Jason, 2000). In order to popularize the academic discourse, we needed to turn the piles of scientific data on their side and look for the human stories contained between the lines. Most writers will tell you that merely giving a creative spin to academic text is often a futile task, because the academic literary voice lacks the idiosyncratic "I"—or "we" in the case of a coauthored book—that anchors much creative nonfiction into the authority of the authors' experience. The objective distance of most academic authors is probably the biggest obstacle to gaining access to trade publishing. In this respect, we had a dubious advantage over academic writers: We had respectively experienced two out of the four topics our book covered. As first and second authors of this book, we respectively had direct experience with chronic fatigue syndrome and recovery from heroin addiction. We had an intimate connection to the topics we were writing about, and we were therefore part of the story we were writing, whether we liked it or not.

Our life experiences were living proof that solutions could be very simple. Namely, they showed that the ability to function productively could be regained thanks in part to a journey through supportive and healing communities. For both of us, this process blended in with ordinary life so seamlessly that we could not make out its outline. Then, writing about it for several years helped us to see what an important role community had played in our recovery. Some academic knowledge was necessary to reveal the nature of a process that could so easily be taken for granted (Jason & Glenwick, 2002). We were in the unique position of understanding what great burdens chronic illness and addictions were to society, while also knowing how we had learned to bear them in our own lives. Had our realization stopped there, we would have started writing memoirs, but there was more for us to see. Thanks to research that pointed to several communal successes, we met scores of people who had found true healing from addictions, chronic medical illness, and mental illness, and even from the debilitating isolation of old age. It wasn't a book about what had worked for the two of us; it was about a kind of solution that saved the lives of many. It could save many more.

This book became a witness to communal solutions designed to relieve suffering among four large groups in American society: people with alcoholism and drug addiction, persons with chronic medical illness, individuals with mental illness, and the elderly. Persons in each of these groups successfully established small communities and gained considerable benefits from their communal lifestyles. In all these healing communities, the most salient feature of success seemed to be that the therapeutic function was woven in the weft of everyday life. This book can be seen as an extension of the old saying, "It takes a community to raise a child," yet in this case, it takes a community to help those with maladies recover.

The awareness that we live in an interconnected world, where the suffering of one person or one group hurts everyone else is now fairly common, but these communities are unique in that they translate this rhetoric into action. By doing so, they discover that in mutuality, helping others becomes a way to help oneself. If it seems simplistic, remember that it is not elementary in terms of its value to anyone who is in need. These self-started communities emphasized the coping resources inherent to each group by gaining strength from numbers. Community members compiled the practical values that insured the survival and growth of their group into a tradition and a history. Stories of unbearable suffering were gradually rewritten into new narratives of lives better lived. In the eyes of the people who experienced this rebirth, it imbued their communities with a quasi-mythical status.

As modern society seems to unravel in unpredictable ways, a remarkably creative solution to ease the suffering and alienation of a few people consists of living together in mutual support. Ironically, in an American culture that is largely defined by the accumulation and distribution of financial wealth, this most effective solution happens to make an efficient use of funds. It may be that those who were left behind in the frantic race for progress hold the effective solution mainstream society needs to regain its balance.

While academic writers have often documented the success of small protective communities of peers as desirable alternatives to institutional treatment, the general public rarely gets to read about them.

Our purpose for correcting this is to provide hope, support, encouragement, and models for those who wish to start such communities and
for individuals who might benefit from new communities and from
existing ones. The first chapter begins by showing how a sense of
community is lacking in contemporary society, which is increasingly
urbanized and polarized by the widening gap between rich and poor.

ACKNOWLEDGMENTS

The authors are deeply appreciative of many colleagues who have helped shape the ideas in this book, including Emory Cowen, Jim Kelly, Bob Newbrough, Stephen Goldston, Ira Iscoe, Murray Levine, Edwin Zolik, and Ken Heller. We are also indebted to our friends who have helped us think through many of the issues in the book, including Daryl Holtz Isenberg, Steve Everett, Harriet Melrose, Eileen Favorite, Roy Cook, Ron and Virginia Christman, Chris Keys, Joe Durlak, John Moritsugu, Roger Weissberg, David Glenwick, Maurice Elias, Ray Lorion, Bob Felner, Bill Berkowitz, Cary Cherness, David Chavis, Jan Gillespie, LaVome Robinson, Susan McMahon, Steve Danish, Irwin Sandler, Ken Maton, Kelly Hazel, Paul Toro, Brian Wilcox, Tom Wolff, Joe Zins, Gary Harper, Carolyn Feis, Stephen Fawcett, Glen White, Mark Matthews, Stevan Hobfoll, Brad Olson, Meg Davis, Josefina Alvarez, Joe Ferrari, Steven Pokorny, Peter Ji, Monica Adams, Doreen Salina, Isiaah Crawford, Michelle Pillen, Vicky Sloan, Tom Soto, Lynne Wagner, Susan Torres-Harding, Renee R. Taylor, David Altman, G. Anne Bogat, Olga Reyes, Cecile Lardon, Jean Hill, Jean Rhodes, and faculty colleagues at DePaul University.

Finally, we appreciate the support and encouragement from the Ragdale Foundation, Thomas Moore, Shaun McNiff, as well as the Greenwood editorial staff, particularly Debbie Carvalko. The authors would also like to thank Paul Malloy, Pam Fischer, Diane Maxwell, Karen Tabari, and Carole Howard for helping coordinate the interviews.

CHAPTER 1

THE SHRINKING OF
COMMUNITY IN AMERICA

Many Americans no longer feel a strong sense of community, and this loss can cause alienation and despair (Dalton, Elias, & Wandersman, 2001). The effects of the breakdown in the sense of community are even worse for those who are forced to live in impersonal institutions where specialists provide medical and psychological care (Michelson & Tepperman, 2003). With the rise of the modern industrial city over the past 150 years, those with mental illness, developmental disabilities, and substance abuse problems have been segregated from society and housed in relatively large and antiseptic institutions (Goffman, 1961). In a growing and disturbing trend, many social service organizations have placed elderly and mentally ill people together in large intermediate care facilities (nursing homes) in recent years. Unfortunately, these dehumanizing settings provide few opportunities for contact with the community, and they rarely provide individuals with the skills or competencies to effectively reenter society (Marion & Coleman, 1991).

Most of those who are discharged from these types of impersonal institutions literally have no place to go. Very few individuals who come out of institutions have the economic resources to obtain mortgages and purchase homes (Smith, Easterlow, Munro, & Turner, 2003). Most no longer have family or friends willing to provide housing, so renting becomes the only option. Without support from family, friends, or a caring community, these vulnerable outcasts from society frequently live alone in rented apartments, and ultimately many become homeless or are reinstitutionalized.

Given the affordable-housing crisis, the situation is exacerbated today for people in need. From 1991 until 1995, the number of low-rent apartments decreased by 900,000, while the number of low-income families increased by 370,000 (U.S. Department of Housing and Urban Development, 1998). In 282 of America's 393 largest metropolitan areas, one-third of renters cannot afford modest one-bedroom apartments (Oxford & Barrett, 1997). The remaining rent options are often grim transient hotels with predatory room rates. These are not optimal settings for maintaining a fragile sobriety or recovering from a crushing depression. Such hotel rooms do not allow cooking, and they are not even safe enough to store wages gathered from meager disability checks to buy a meal at the corner diner. Not only is this happening to people released from mental hospitals and substance abuse treatment settings, but also to the chronically ill and the elderly (Jason & Kobayashi, 1995).

Many live alone and isolated, some with chronic illnesses or disabilities. Both research and common sense attribute vulnerabilities to our environment and its inadequate sense of community. Without the support of community, disabling illnesses that could otherwise be managed become life threatening.

Whether it is physical illness, mental illness, old age, or substance abuse that brings about poverty, it is much harder in a society that lacks a sense of community. Because it is much larger than we are, the current situation seems overwhelming. We have fallen out of a fundamental relationship with everything, and we feel lost (Purpel, 1989). Where do we look for a remedy? Is the answer located inside ourselves or outside?

First- and Second-Order Change

One reason many traditional approaches have not worked well is that they create what psychologists know as a first-order change. A first-order change is a short-term change that (1) influences the individual without changing the community within which that individual lives, and (2) leads social service providers to allocate increasing amounts of resources toward the same, ineffective interventions (Watzlawick, Weakland, & Fisch, 1974). First-order interventions often make worse the crises they were originally intended to resolve. For example, traditional inpatient treatment programs for substance abuse are ineffective because individuals are almost always discharged to high-risk environments, and these are the very environments that contributed to the substance abuse problem in the first place (Jason, Olson et al., 2003–2004).

In contrast to this, second-order change influences the individual, his or her social network, and all other components of the environment that can contribute to a particular problem (Watzlawick et al., 1974). Second-order thinking involves "finding ways that persons with disorders may help each other, or ways that persons with disorders may be enabled to assume greater autonomy in managing their lives" (Dalton et al., 2001, p. 9).

This book is about these types of second-order change: social environments where individuals are surrounded with love, support, and caring. The havens presented in later chapters provide a stunning alternative to first-order interventions, as they help build communities and provide long-term support for those most in need. But first, we need to examine some of the reasons for the breakdown in the sense of community.

The Need for Community

Spretnak (1991) traced our contemporary vulnerabilities to origins predating the Industrial Revolution. She believed that many maladies of our modern world were in fact consequences of our tendency to control and dominate the forces of nature rather than live in a respectful balance with nature. For Spretnak, a breakdown in the sense of community was inevitable once the larger forces of nature were considered engulfing and devouring. Laguna Pueblo and Sioux writer Paula Gunn Allen (1992, p. 60) completed Spretnak's historical exposé with an essential definition of health as "wholeness" and disease as "a condition of division and separation from the harmony of the whole." If we feel a sacred sense of connection and respect for our world, we are less likely to dominate the forces of nature, excessively pollute, overpopulate, and threaten our very survival. Whereas Spretnak can reconstruct the historical narrative of disease in the modern world, Allen's native worldview reveals that the root of illness consists of a tendency of Western thinking to separate ourselves from nature. It follows rather logically that community—which unites rather than divides—would attract healing. Grassroots communities could transform the worldview of their members from alienation to wholeness by creating havens that would invite health and healing and counteract disease.

Many of our contemporary social problems can be traced to the erosion of values caused by popular entertainment media, to the loss of faith brought on by political machinations of government, to the loss of meaning that came with the ritualization of religion, and to the widening gap between the rich and the poor. We start feeling numb as we watch the hearts of these social maelstroms collapsing on centers of fear, rage, and isolation. But the situation is not hopeless; we believe that the discipline needed to confront these core issues is still available. We are not powerless.

So far, the solutions put in place to address the needs of people with addiction, old age, mental illness, and chronic medical ailments have usually failed to respect the depth and complexity of the problems, and these traditional programs have fallen short of the comprehensive antidotes that are needed. Local, state, and federal mental and health care programs have often failed to address the void at the heart of so many of our social problems: the loss of a true sense of community.

The dwindling resources allocated to social service programs are not sufficient to address the myriad of problems our country faces at home. If our resources are to have any real effect, we must invest them in the creation of real community. We believe that policymakers who allocate resources to social programs and the traditional social service systems that use those resources have been unable to develop the comprehensive programming that is needed. We assume that this is due to a lack of understanding about the crucial value of community. This book presents a comprehensive approach to developing and sustaining a psychological sense of community.

The approaches highlighted in this book share several characteristics. First, they address all the needs of participants. Second, these solutions are not expensive, so that they can be easily replicated in communities across the country. Third and most important, these programs are effective in creating a psychological sense of community. By this we mean that they help stimulate a process by which participants can increase their commitment to their programs, as well as enhance their sense of connectedness and responsibility to one another.

This book takes an innovative approach toward contemporary problems. The programs profiled are here to serve as models for real and substantive change, and they could help us rebuild the antiquated and ineffective system of social and health care services.

Causes of Community Loss

Modern thinkers have suggested that for many individuals the meaning of life has been tied to acquiring increasing income and status, yet few are satisfied with this utter self-absorption (Bellah, Madsen, Sullivan, Swidler, & Tipton, 1985). These symbols and goals might be part of the problem of society today. If loss of community or relatedness is an underlying root of many modern problems (Sarason, 1974), the understanding of its history might contribute to its resolution.

According to Morgan (1942), throughout history people lived in communal dwellings. It was within the village that people helped each other, not out of charity but because it was the natural way of life. Relations between people grew spontaneously from mutual affection, customs, and traditions. In other words, the need for interconnection was selected rather organically, because it made survival more likely. At times, village life was burdened with narrowness and provincialism; however, the positive features of mutual respect, working together for common ends, and neighborliness were strong features that provided nurturing and meaning.

Over the last 150 years, some sociologists and anthropologists have noticed a change in values within our culture (Jason, 1997). Prior to the Industrial Revolution, people had specific roles in crafts and farming, and these jobs provided meaning to their lives. As more and more people moved from the village to the cities, the long-term bonds with the land were severed, and some family and community traditions began to weaken. Modern societies began to feature formal organizations, contracts, and legislature. Etzioni (1993) believes that many Americans have a strong sense of entitlement but a weak sense of obligation to serve their communities. Our present modern societies have greater individual freedom, but the cost has been a decline in the human ability to relate and in community spirit and neighborliness (McLaughlin & Davidson, 1985). Stein (1960) has traced the effects of urbanization, industrialization, and bureaucratization on the transformation of America. In reviewing the work of others, Stein concluded that industrialization killed the old sense of coherence and satisfaction people gained from contributing their craft to their community, and replaced it with a new emphasis on competition and individual achievement.

When culture, rituals, and customs began to decline, people stopped participating in the larger community. As values and beliefs changed, people became estranged from each other and increasingly focused on the individual (Bellah et al., 1985). In the 1940s and 1950s, people aspired to an ever-rising standard of living, which in turn justified grueling industrial work roles. In this new society (Stein, 1960), people felt alienated and isolated, and the local community ceased to be a place that mattered. Life transitions like birth, adulthood, marriage, and death were minimized or performed perfunctorily by impersonal social agencies, schools, or churches.

Yet, many people in urban settings have been able to integrate old and new traditions, and to develop a sense of community. Many individuals in industrial societies continue to hold the traditions, values, and myths that effectively guided their predecessors. Many small towns in America continue to have many elements of a caring community. In this respect, the way many modern Native Americans live in urban environments is interesting, because it proves that it is possible to succeed in two diametrically opposed cultures. Traditional tribal culture defines success by how much can be given away, while Western culture defines it by how much one has accumulated. The higher one progresses in positions of leadership in Western culture, the more ego one develops, and the less modesty and humility one shows. In contrast, many Native American tribal leaders have the fewest material possessions because they were able to give away the most.

Contemporary Native American tribal people hold dear the values of their traditions, but are challenged to implement them in Western society. Those who negotiate the tricky business of succeeding in both worlds all say the same thing. They make as much money as possible in the Western world and sponsor as many doings as they can in the tribal world. This illustrates how even a community that holds values contrary to the dominant world can exist without having to change the entire world first.

The concept of community finds its origins and its ideal in tribal culture, and its Western applications have grown pale in comparison. Western values of individual pursuit, competitiveness, and narcissism corrupt the communal process at the individual level and spread out in concentric circles. Community in the traditional tribal world is continually enriched by the impulse to give to others, whereas community in Western culture is too often just another unit of competition and self-aggrandizement, next to corporations and political states. However, alternative viewpoints do exist within Western thought. For example, in *A Theory of Justice*, Rawls (1971) maintains that members of a society need to be provided with basic rights (i.e., freedom of speech, conscience, peaceful assembly) and more or less equal opportunities. Rawls emphatically states that redistribution of resources can only occur within a state when the redistribution of these resources benefits the most disadvantaged members.

Many of the concepts within this book fit well within the voluntary simplicity movement. This term was first popularized in Elgin's (1981) book *Voluntary Simplicity*, which referred to a simpler lifestyle by reducing consumption in order to help conserve Earth's dwindling resources, help contend with a burgeoning world population, and better deal with a growing gap between the rich and the poor. The havens that we profile in this book are very much examples of this voluntary simplicity movement, and they are available to serve as models for substantive and lasting change.

In this book, we do not use the term *community* as the buzzword that is so often found in corporations, but as a practical solution to very thorny problems. True communities in the Western world—where members give back more to the community than they keep for themselves—require such an attitudinal change that they are usually created under some sort of duress. Life-threatening addiction, debilitating chronic illness, alienating mental disease, and the loneliness of old age seem so far to be the most effective motivating factors for creating true communities in Western culture.

This book is intended to show the public at large that true community, if it were found more widely, would yield preventive benefits for society at large. However, many individuals in our mobile, industrial society lack a community of reference, with its attending belief system and customs.

The declining sense of community might have also been indirectly reinforced by the scientific revolution (Jason, 1997). Although we can appreciate the enormous changes science brought, including the sophisticated treatment of diseases and more efficient agricultural methods, the passion to perceive and understand nature might have contributed to a crisis of the belief systems and values in some people. As science prospered, some began to believe that intellectual prowess and achievement were the only symbols of success (Bartel & Guskin, 1971), and others, including many existentialists (Sartre, 1956), proposed that religions and myths that had once guided people through their lives were antiquated and no longer relevant. Campbell (1949) maintained that many modern-day problems were a result of the lack of nurturing and validating rituals and images that once gave people's lives meaning.

Many have found balance between the demands of modern life and the organic process of relationship. It is to these people that we might look for clues to strengthening our relatedness to each other and the world in a larger sense. These communities may not have surmounted all the problems of modern society, but they are working for their members in deep, meaningful ways.

During the early 1800s, the Quakers became one of the first groups to establish these types of healing communities. The Quakers invited mental patients to a house in the country surrounded by natural beauty, where they were treated with warmth and compassion. Additionally, in Gheel, Belgium, for the past few hundred years, individuals with serious mental disorders and mental retardation were allowed to live on farms. The Gheel system has been regarded as one of the most humane methods of dealing with persistent mental illness. Finally, Murphy (1982) found low rates of schizophrenia in the Tonga Islands in the South Pacific and in a collectivist, pacifist Hutterite sect in western Canada. While excessive individualism and personal insecurity seemed to foster schizophrenia elsewhere, the high degrees of social harmony emphasized in these communities were associated with lower rates of schizophrenia.

In the communities we describe in this book, we saw ordinary citizens and members of disenfranchised communities demonstrating the tenacity and creativity of many individuals working together, mounting effective efforts against disability, illness, addiction, aging, and isolation. We found that a psychological sense of community was the energizing force in all these groups. What can we learn from these communities, and how can we support others in their efforts to create community? How can we interact with them in supportive, educational, mutually beneficial ways without interfering with their course? In essence, how can we better understand what processes underlie the success of these communities and support similar success in other communities? We asked ourselves these questions as we began to research the communities featured in this book.

Upcoming Chapters

In order to generate the following chapters, we interviewed individuals who were able to overcome drug and alcohol addiction, elderly hopelessness, mental illness, and chronic medical ailments. We sought to understand their stories just as naturalists look closely at the world of nature to uncover the mystery and truths of life. Our job was to reveal beauty, peer deep into the complexities, and discover realities that could become inspirations for our own lives.

Chapter 2 features Bob, Jill, Mike, and others who became addicted to drugs and alcohol and for years were unable to stay sober due to the high visibility of alcohol and drugs, pressure from peers and families to continue getting high, lack of support, and economic hardship. Fortunately, their journeys led them to grassroots efforts by recovering addicts to establish hundreds of remarkably different recovery homes across the country. These small, self-supported, self-governed communities allowed them to finally find long-term sobriety.

In chapter 3, Trudy and Myron escape the grim prospects of nursing-home life by choosing instead to spend many more happy years in the familylike community of H.O.M.E. (Housing and Maintenance Opportunity for the Elderly). H.O.M.E. lets residents keep their dignity as they get older.

Chapter 4 tells the story of Bruce, Sylvia, and Tim, who are among many adults suffering from mental illness. They have greatly decreased their rates of hospitalization by moving into the GROW community. GROW provides true home life and psychological safety for 16 people who find healing from mental illness in mutual support. The attention that GROW's success attracts from state regulators illustrates the counterproductive nature of the dominant mental health system.

Chapter 5 reveals the difficult lives of people with chronic medical ailments. Community solutions that relieve the suffering caused by addictions, aging, and mental illness elude people with chronic medical ailments, particularly those afflicted with the debilitating condition of chronic fatigue syndrome (CFS). Without the energy to advocate for themselves, CFS sufferers like Jim and Angela find that the community-building strategies that work for others do not work for them. Jim and Angela are nevertheless able to craft their own healing journeys by seeking out bits and pieces of community from a variety of places.

Chapter 6 explores other lessons in community healing. The value of successful healing communities is that they constitute a more efficient use of funding. If public health funds were allocated more equitably, as a function of a program's true efficiency rather than the size of its budget, health needs would be met more fully and for more people. True community only happens with time, most often on a small scale. In order to grow, a community needs to be identified and nurtured through supportive research and corresponding policy. When we collaborate with community groups, we become a more caring and humane society with the means to provide decent living conditions for all our citizens.

CHAPTER 2

MORE THAN A BLESSING

About 42 percent of Americans report having used an illegal drug at least once during their lifetimes. Whether you have never used street drugs, did it once, several times, or still use them today, you should know that the cost of illegal drug use to our society is $160 billion (Office of National Drug Control Policy, 2003). Alcohol abuse and drug dependence are also extremely costly to society. It is estimated that the average employee abusing drugs works at 67 percent of his or her potential. Alcoholism also exacts a tremendous price for the 4.5 percent to 10.0 percent of the population it affects (8% to 14% of men and 1% to 6% of women). Chronic alcohol and drug consumption often leads to people losing their jobs, their homes, and their families (Jason, Davis, Ferrari, & Bishop, 2001). It also leads to poor health (75% of all deaths attributed to alcoholism are due to cirrhosis of the liver; other diseases are caused by poor living conditions, malnutrition, and further abuses of the body). Women who consume alcohol during pregnancy run the risk of giving birth to babies with fetal alcohol syndrome, which includes malformation of the head and brain. In fact, the leading cause of mental retardation in the Western world today is alcohol consumption by pregnant women. Well over half of crimes and motor vehicle accidents are related to alcohol use, which has been found to contribute to violence and aggression.

The high prevalence and enormous costs of alcoholism to both the individual and society, whether measured in terms of health or economics, illustrate how much is at stake if we find a successful response to it. A review of the literature on the effectiveness of substance abuse treatment indicates that many men and women relapse within one year of completion of an inpatient treatment that includes immediate detoxification with adjacent therapies provided by medical professionals, and that 52 percent to 75 percent drop out during treatment (Montgomery, Miller, & Tonigan, 1993). After treatment for substance abuse in a hospital-based treatment program, a therapeutic community, or a recovery home, many patients return to a high-risk environment or a stressful family situation. Then, many relapse. As many an addict will tell you, "If you keep going to the barbershop, eventually, you'll get your hair cut." Returning to these settings without a network of people to support abstinence increases chances of a relapse, which is why substance abuse recidivism following treatment is high for both men and women. Under modern managed care, private and public sector inpatient substance abuse facilities have reduced their services dramatically. In addition, the social environment in which patients are discharged has great influence in hindering or helping them remain sober and drug free. Thus, there is a tremendous need to develop, evaluate, and expand lower-cost communal options for substance abuse patients. The social environment to which our patients are discharged represents a critical variable that is likely to influence our ultimate success in helping patients remain sober and drug free.

The Oxford House Story

The Oxford Houses that we describe in this chapter are large homes located in safe residential neighborhoods that are rented by eight or nine roommates (Jason et al., 2001). The houses are unsupervised and run solely by the recovering addicts, who manage everything from bank accounts to cooking. Paul Molloy founded Oxford House in the Washington, D.C., area in 1975. He had worked as a Senate committee staff member from 1967 to 1972, during which time he was an active alcoholic. In 1975 he left his government position and began his recovery from substance abuse. While living in a halfway house in Montgomery County, Maryland, he saw 12 fellow house members forced to leave the house because they had reached six months residency, the maximum length of stay. Of these 12 men, 11 relapsed within 30 days. Molloy and the other residents then received word that the halfway house had lost its funding and would close within 30 days. After considerable confusion and exchange of ideas with members of the Alcoholics Anonymous (AA) community, Molloy and five other residents decided to take over the lease for the house themselves. Although they initially had wanted to hire a staff person, they were unable to do so because of the cost. They decided to run the house on their own in a democratic fashion. They named their community Oxford House after the Oxford Group, a religious organization that influenced the founders of Alcoholics Anonymous.

In discussing the way the house should operate, local AA members urged the residents to keep it simple. Many residents had disliked the rules of the old halfway house, but they agreed that one positive aspect had been the enforcement of sobriety through the immediate eviction of residents who used alcohol or other drugs. A plan for organizing the house emerged from these discussions. Members voted to repeal the six-month time limit, abolished curfews, and established a few simple rules of conduct: operate democratically, have members pay rent and do all assigned chores, and stay sober. Deviation from these rules is cause for immediate eviction. Consequently, there are no professional staff members at Oxford Houses and all costs of the program are covered by residents.

Six months after the first Oxford House was formed, it had accumulated enough resources to begin a second. Members of the second house, in turn, worked to form a third. Within 13 years, and without the aid of outside funding, the number of Oxford House homes grew to more than 20. In July 1988 Congressman Edward Madigan asked residents of Oxford House for ideas for legislation that would help promote the Oxford House concept nationwide. After residents testified about their experiences, new legislation was introduced to help spread this innovative approach to recovery. A provision within the Federal Anti-Drug Abuse Act of 1988 mandated that each of the 50 states establish a revolving fund of $100,000 to be used for $4,000 loans to cover startup costs for each self-run and self-supported recovery house. Between 1988 and 2002 the number of Oxford House homes replicating this innovative community-based model has increased to more than 850 in some 200 cities across the country, providing a safe place to recover for thousands of addicts and alcoholics each year. Considering that 56 percent to 72 percent of Oxford House members have police records, it is not just their happiness that is at stake in their successful rehabilitation. Your own tranquillity could depend on it as well.

Over time, Molloy and the original founders created nine traditions—benchmarks that ensured that Oxford Houses were the homes of alcoholics and addicts in recovery rather than people who had relapsed. Tradition one established the initial goal of providing housing and rehab support for alcoholics and addicts who wanted to stop using.

Tradition two insured that all houses were run on a democratic basis. To this end, house officers could not be elected for more than six-month terms. Molloy tells the story of the first decision he and his roommates reached democratically: whether to buy a mechanical can opener or an electrical one. After a very long discussion, they sent someone to buy the electrical one, and admired it for a while on the kitchen counter. It stood there as a reassuring symbol of their ability to reach a decision in an orderly fashion.

Tradition three guaranteed that no members could ever be asked to leave without cause—using drugs or alcohol, disrupting the home, or falling behind on bill payments. Molloy, who had seen many people relapse due to a six-months limit in shelters, ended up living at Oxford House for two and a half years. Some members have even lived at an Oxford House for the rest of their lives.

Tradition four emphasized the lack of official affiliation with Alcoholics Anonymous or Narcotics Anonymous, while stressing the importance of attending 12-step meetings. Successful Oxford House members typically attend three or four meetings a week.

Tradition five made each Oxford House autonomous in terms of decision making, except in matters affecting other Oxford Houses or the organization as a whole. Tradition six specified that each house must be financially self-supported, except for startup money, which has to come from a loan.

Another tradition—seven—ensures that the house is not taken over by anyone in particular, and that it can be democratically run by all its members at weekly house meetings. It indicates that Oxford House is forever nonprofessional. A house can still contract with professionals if it deems that doing so would enhance the process of recovery, and some members receive professional services like psychotherapy outside of the home.

In order to minimize ego trips, tradition eight placed the principles of Oxford House before personality. This is why homes have always been rented, never owned. Finally, tradition nine encouraged departing members in good standing to become associate members and to keep in touch with their alumni house.

New Oxford House residents are required to abstain from drugs and alcohol for 30 days before they can move in. Even then, the 2001 Oxford House Manual calls for an 80 percent majority vote by the residents, and members must pay their portion of the rent, do their share of chores, refrain from disturbing the unity of the house, and abstain from drugs and alcohol. Oxford Houses don't usually have money to spare for frivolities, but their budgets are totally self-sufficient. Without any supervision, without the bureaucratic inertia that accompanies government funding, Oxford Houses are able to grow independently to become stable and healthy homes.

In this chapter, you will meet Bob, Jill, and others (all names have been changed to protect privacy), who after years of exhausting relapses and discouraging stays in detox centers, finally recovered from heroin and alcohol addiction by moving into the community of Oxford House. Unlike other treatment settings, Oxford House is a network of hundreds of inconspicuous houses rented by addicts who are able to stay sober without supervision. Oxford House residents maintain much higher sobriety rates than participants in traditional recovery programs. The network of sober houses is democratically self-administered, financially independent, and growing steadily. In order to understand why Oxford House is such a good model, we must first consider the story of some of the addicts who found clean and sober lives there.

Bob: Living Life on Life's Terms

For 26 years, Bob's drug of choice had been heroin, but if you sat down with him over coffee, he'd tell you he wasn't all that picky about which drug to use, as long as it made him feel like somebody else. Bob is very candid about this now that he's kicked the habit; he'll even joke about it. Before that, though, you'd have gotten a different story from Bob—that is, assuming you were willing to go find him living in the abandoned shell of a car on the South Side of Chicago.

Bob grew up in the projects, a cluster of 13-story high-rises on the West Side of Chicago, where he found that "ninety-nine percent of the youth used some type of drug." His less than ideal family life included an alcoholic father who urinated over everything in the tiny apartment when he came home drunk—he often mistook a closet for the bathroom—and then picked fights with Bob or anybody else he could lay his hands on. Home was hardly a haven from the dangers that lurked in the immense building's stairwells. Bob lived in fear of trying to get home safely, only to get pummeled by his drunken father. Understandably, doing drugs helped him escape his calamitous family life and the feelings of inadequacy it engendered.

Bob now thinks he smoked his first marijuana joint because he didn't like himself and didn't have a sense of belonging. Smoking pot gave him an escape from his private hell, and fooled him into an illusory and temporary sense of freedom. School wasn't a priority, so nothing discouraged him from experimenting with some of the widely available drugs. Bob quickly went from smoking marijuana to guzzling cough syrup for the codeine. He developed a preference for downer drugs. They provided him with the relaxation and mellowness he so desperately needed, and led him quite naturally to heroin, which gave him everything he was looking for. A girlfriend introduced Bob to heroin, and he feared loosing her if he didn't try it. Bob had not yet reached his twenty-fourth birthday. His need to fit in overpowered his self-preservation instincts. He admired the way guys stood around at the pool hall, leaning against walls, very still, with their heads cocked to one side, cigarettes dangling from their lower lips. He liked the way long ashes hung from their cigarettes while they scrutinized a game through a haze of smoke, breaking off suddenly when they finally moved for their turn.

The "three dollar buttons" Bob first started using were inexpensive enough. The little gelatin capsules were filled with heroin that had been cut, but for only three bucks, Bob could get high for a few hours. He used heroin for a couple of days, then abstained for a few days, but he quickly developed painful withdrawal symptoms. Taking the advice of his drug buddies, he snorted more of it, which of course relieved his symptoms. Bob didn't ask himself how much damage he was doing to his body and soul; he just knew how much heroin it took to make his life bearable. As his tolerance increased, he had to use more heroin, slowly but surely replacing one nightmare with another.

The cost of his daily high steadily rose from $20 to $400. This meant he had to spend most of his day stealing merchandise from department stores and returning it, without a receipt, in a mall across town, until he collected his $400.

"It was a lot of work to get high," Bob later said to us, thinking back.

He explained how the $400 he needed each day to support his habit really only got him around $40 worth of heroin, because the stuff for sale on the street had been cut so many times before he got it.

He began selling heroin to support his habit, but that proved to be a lousy way to make money because he became his own best customer and consumed all the profits.

"Monkeys can't sell bananas," Bob reminded us as we listened to his life story.

The heroin met such a deep need for appeasement and belonging for Bob that he didn't feel normal without it, and he began to accept the thought that he would eventually die because of it. He tried to quit cold turkey and lay shivering in cold sweats for days, with lymph nodes the size of pool balls, crawling to the commode doubled over with diarrhea, wishing he would die. But even after enduring all this, he still returned to shooting up. There were many other times he wanted to stop, but as time went by, he felt increasingly unable to do so. Slowly, Bob realized he had a disease that he could not control. For many years, no one noticed, and he found himself caught between his addiction and his ability to conceal it. His shoplifting routine got bolder and more careless. He would stroll right into a department store, pile a bunch of expensive items by the door until it looked like enough stuff, then just run out with it. It was as if he wanted to get caught and arrested—as a way of asking for help. He began to wonder how he might die. Would he overdose alone behind an alley Dumpster, or would he get shot in the back by a security guard as he ran out of a store? He knew one thing for sure: He would die soon, like many of his addicted friends, and his death would be a direct result of using heroin. The worst part was that he felt like he was dead already.

As tends to happen with addicts, Bob's losses started accumulating. His marriage had disintegrated—he had married young—and he had not seen his son in a while. Even his material possessions dwindled, as every object got pawned for a fix. The only thing he owned was a broken-down car that hadn't run in months. It was still parked where the engine had died, on an out-of-the-way side street, and he lived in it. Around mid-morning, he emerged from the wreck, stinking from going days without a shower, and embarked on yet another day of stealing. On those days, he rode the bus to kill time and to think about a way to score his next bag. Then one day, Bob bumped into a former acquaintance during the bus ride. The man was one of his former "get high buddies," but he looked different; his skin and his eyes were clearer than Bob remembered. The man wore clean clothes and looked well. Bob probably sounded envious as he asked the man questions and found out that he had been in a detox program. Over the years, Bob had met others who had been through rehab, but most continued to use after finishing these programs. If I go to a 30-day program, Bob thought, it would only keep me clean for a few days. He wondered what it was about this man that had kept him clean once he had left rehab.

Unfortunately, Bob's pessimism was realistic; inpatient detoxification programs do not work for most addicts. Few seem to be able to stay clean more than a few days once they leave the program and return to temptations on the outside. Bob knew that drugs were slowly killing him, and a faint voice inside was begging him to give it up. Though he was reluctant to go to a treatment program, he knew his life of stealing was hopeless. He didn't care if he got caught because he was by now imprisoned by his addiction. The prospect of death was no deterrent either, since he felt dead already. He was moved by his encounter with the man who had successfully quit drugs, so he decided to go into treatment in spite of his doubts.

At age 45, after using drugs for over 20 years, Bob finally checked himself into a 30-day detox and treatment program. The first thing he noticed was how much he enjoyed being with people who talked coherently, who dressed neatly, and who smelled good. This first stay filled Bob with the hope that he had escaped his inner prison. Unfortunately, getting detoxed and attending Narcotics Anonymous meetings left him hungry for what he needed. His level of hope began to evaporate.

"There is a difference between being clean and sober and being in recovery," Bob explained. "Even just going to a 12-step program like Alcoholics Anonymous wasn't enough. It still felt like there was some elements missing."

Bob could have the drugs purged out of his body, and he could stay clean, but his underlying thinking was the same. The program provided a way for him to cleanse his body of street drugs, but it had barely begun to scratch the surface of what drove him to drugs in the first place. Without a deeper level of change, he was at risk of relapsing.

When Bob first got out of treatment, he lived with two other guys who had been in treatment with him, but they soon began getting high again, so Bob moved out in a hurry and went to stay with his girlfriend, Sheri. Once he moved in with her, Bob slipped back into the old, abusive patterns of relating that had caused stress and pain in his past relationships. Unable to put himself in her shoes, he made unreasonable demands on Sheri, like having free access to her car. Once again, Bob felt swept away in a current he could not control. It was "his way or the highway," as he puts it.

"Even clean, I still felt like I wasn't real proud of what I was," Bob explained.

Bob found unexpected solace in a conversation he had with his friend Erick, who was having similar problems relating to his girlfriend. Erick had decided to move into an alcohol and drug abuse recovery home he had heard about, Oxford House, in part to escape from the difficulties he was having with his girlfriend. Oxford House recovery homes had two rules: Residents could take no alcohol or drugs, and they had to pay rent. There were no professional staff members in the home, residents could stay as long as they wanted, and they ran the house democratically. Intrigued, Bob decided to follow his friend, and they roomed together at an Oxford House.

It didn't take long for Bob's relational style to be confronted head on. On his second day there, one of the house residents told Bob he was codependent. Codependency is a cluster of character traits that leads people to live their own lives through the lives of others. Bob had learned it early as a way to survive the abuse he suffered at the hands of his father. It is usually a character hallmark for most addicts, and it explains the difficulty addicts have in taking responsibility, making their own decisions, and being direct and honest. Bob accepted that label with difficulty, but everyday life at the Oxford House gradually showed him through experience that the resident was right. In the past, Bob had successfully deflected such confrontations, but his defensive skills were useless here. Unlike treatment settings, there was no authority figure, no one to blame for his problems.

Upon coming into the Oxford House, Bob began to learn how to express himself without feeling shame. As Bob developed enough trust in his roommate Erick, he unburdened himself with painful stories he had carried around for years. For the first time in his life, he had been allowed to put down his heavy load and take a look at it.

"These were guys who I felt more love from than my actual family members," Bob said in amazement. "We are still there for one another. And we go through the same things that people go through with their real families."

Granted, Bob had many losses to grieve, some from the violent family he grew up in, others from years of drug use and self-deception, but it should be noted here that few of us ever experience what it is like to live with others this honestly. We all have shortcomings that often do not get addressed in the way Oxford House residents confront theirs. Bob learned to cry and also confided in other residents in the home. He didn't hold anything back, and for the first time in his life, complete honesty was the norm. As Bob slowly learned how to express his emotions, he found room in his heart to comfort others. He began to develop the ability to have compassion for somebody else besides himself. Just wanting to help somebody else without having an ulterior motive was a new experience. When Erick became despondent over difficulties with his girlfriend, he would get into a fetal position with his thumb in his mouth and cry. Bob would be there to console him, unashamed to cry with another grown man. That was something Bob never had experienced prior to living in an Oxford House.

Bob explained that, although Oxford House offered a unique combination of mutual support, safety, and freedom, it also required him to fulfill responsibilities.

"Oxford House is a stepping stone," he said. "It's a way to learn to live life on life's terms."

Bob found it easier to learn through the example of his peers than from anything treatment staff members had ever told him. The longer Bob lived at the Oxford House, the more he gained a sense of appreciation for the responsibilities of everyday life. To pay his share of the weekly rent, he had to get a job right away. Being able to pay his own rent gave Bob a new sense of independence.

"It's not that I'm proud of it, because it's what I was supposed to be doing the whole time anyway," Bob said modestly, tilting his head to one side. Looking down at his shoes, he added, "I regret the time I lost, because there's nothing I can do to get it back."

Haunted by past losses, Bob found his salvation in the present moment, one day at a time. When we interviewed him, he liked to contemplate the daily routine of work at his job and chores at home.

"I know now that all those things I do during the day are important. Those things are what my sobriety is made of. I try to keep a good balance going."

Communal living at the Oxford House nurtured healthy relationships between residents. Bob found that everyone else in his home supported his sobriety. It was a stark contrast to the high-crime neighborhood where he used to live, where dealers stopped him at every corner and offered to sell him heroin. The anonymity that shielded his daily heroin use for years was absent at the Oxford House. The men he shared the house with all knew what he was up to. As Bob gained self-confidence among his roommates, he allowed himself to relate to them more openly. Gradually, the helping relationship between them became mutual. By helping others, he helped himself.

"The most important thing I've learned at Oxford House is that it's not all about me. When I was using, it was all me! Me! Me!" Bob said.

"Now, I look beyond myself, and I do the things that I'm supposed to be doing. That's all."

More important changes were beginning to occur in the way Bob related to others. He found himself increasingly able to handle conflict without taking everything so personally. Bob learned that conflicts were part of healthy relationships.

"We still have arguments," Bob pointed out. "And we get past it and we still care for one another. There is one guy in my house, and we battle with each other like cats and dogs, but no matter what I'm going through, and no matter where I am, and no matter what he's doing, he'll drop what he is doing to make sure that I'm OK. And I do the same thing with him."

Bob could also accept defeat without turning it into personal failure. He had moved from being closed-minded and self-centered to being open to and tolerant of other viewpoints.

"I took offense at practically everything," Bob said to us, shaking his head.

The mutuality and honesty of relationships inside Oxford House gradually forced Bob to redefine his sense of self and to acknowledge the connections that formed between him and others. Slowly, he learned that their feelings were as important as his own.

"It is OK that I am not always right, and it is a good thing that I am wrong sometimes because it gives me an opportunity to grow," Bob pondered. "I can be wrong about something and learn from it."

Bob had been living there for only a few months, and already he could trace his progression from the limbo he felt after the last 30-day detox, to his regular attendance at 12-step meetings, and finally his landing at Oxford House. This last step felt like a huge leap.

To Bob, this new life was "more than just a blessing, it was a miracle from God." Indeed, seen from the perspective of his life before Oxford House, his new relationships must have seemed angelic.

As he talked to us, Bob's eyebrows raised all the way up as he tried to convey his awe. "Here is this person I don't have to expect anything from and he doesn't have to expect anything from me, and we are willing to be there for each other!"

Bob started to turn his new ability to have compassion on his own past, realizing how self-centered and demanding he had been in his relationships. His mind was opening just enough to let him understand that being self-centered was the core of his disease.

"When I was using, the mentality that I had was I would steal it from you before you stole it from me. Let me trick you out of something before you might trick it out of me. Let me physically hurt you before you hurt me."

Bob described Oxford House like "a society within a society." It allowed him to take an honest look at himself and others and to develop his level of awareness. When we interviewed Bob, he had lived in an Oxford House for six years, and though he had both inflicted and felt tremendous pain, he was grateful for what the journey has taught him. He understood he needed to catch up on his grieving in order to grow as a person. Bob had a deeply reverent attitude toward the Oxford House way of life and the values it reestablished for him. It not only saved his life, but it also gave him a quality of life he never knew existed. Although he never uttered the words *sacred* and *spirituality*, they were implied in the way he told us his story. Bob derived joy by transcending his idea of self, by helping someone else. He didn't seem to mind that some of this kindness was lost on others, or sometimes anonymous, for what mattered most to him was the joy he felt inside.

From learning to relate all over again with the extended family of Oxford House, Bob reconstructed his relationship with his own family, his estranged wife, and his children.

"I spent a lot of time playing with the children in and around the house, and I became sort of a father figure," he said. "I was a pretty lousy father when I was using. That time at Oxford House was how I learned to be a better parent."

Alumni: Staying Connected

Friendships developed in Oxford Houses often grow into lifelong relationships. Even two years after she left Oxford House to live in her own apartment, Jill often drove to her alumni house to help current residents and also just to visit.

When we met with Jill, she had known Bob for five years. She explained that the recovering community was tight-knit.

"There are probably three Narcotics Anonymous meetings a day, seven days a week going on within a five-mile radius," Jill said. She told the story of a new woman in her house who called in tears because she had missed her bus and didn't want to be late for her first day at work. Jill called a friend at another house near the woman, and the woman got a ride to work.

Jill squinted slightly and her voice quickened when she told us that story, because she knew the value of a support network. She also knew the ordeal of mending alone the pieces of a life ruined by addiction.

By her own account, Jill had been an addict since the age of nine, when she started taking caffeine pills. Her mother popped amphetamine pills like they were mints, and her father regularly drank himself into a violent rage. To make matters worse, he was a Golden Gloves boxer. Out of the blue, he would just walk by and punch Jill in the head. Jill grew up cringing every time he walked by. Her father also used her mother as a punching bag, and they took turns getting one black eye after another, unless he elected to strangle her, which was another favorite move of his. Jill's dad once kicked her down the stairs. Another time he broke her collarbone and elbow.

"Back then we had these rules that you don't say anything to anyone outside the family, and you don't have any feelings," Jill said, remembering. "But I occasionally did call the police."

Her dad never got arrested because he would leave for several days before the cops got there, and her mom never pressed charges.

Outside of Jill's home life, everyone saw only the trappings of a harmonious family. Jill was actually an altar girl and attended Catholic school. "Why are these things happening to me?" Jill thought, wondering if she had been adopted or born into the wrong family. She tried to be as good as possible, to get love and validation from others outside the family.

"When I was nine," Jill said. "My mom got a bottle of champagne for New Year's Eve, but when my dad didn't come home, I remember saying, 'Well, I'll have a drink with you, Mom.'" Jill ended up drinking almost the entire bottle. "I got this warm feeling and everything seemed to disappear, and I had my first blackout."

Jill's mother had three jobs, and she had her first heart attack at the age of 36. Jill took care of the house—shopping, cooking, cleaning, and doing the laundry. With her mom in and out of the hospital, nine-year-old Jill was pushed into a surrogate mother role for her younger brother and sister. In order to cope with her dad's violent outbursts, Jill began drinking beer. After guzzling the beer, she would not feel the pain as much, and she would not feel as lonely. One or two cans of Schlitz did the trick, and Jill looked forward to the warm feeling every couple of days. She liked feeling tipsy but never out of control. Jill's parents said that it was okay for her to drink as long as she did it in the house, but they asked her to be discrete about it.

Jill tried to stay away from the house as much as possible, knowing that anything could happen to her at home. She went to Mass almost every day in the church next door, and worked with the nuns in the adjoining convent.

Once in a while, she traveled to Wisconsin with her dad, to a bar owned by friends of his. Wisconsin applied laws on drinking age liberally, letting 14-year-olds drink as long as they were accompanied by a parent. So Jill would sip on her drink while her dad got hammered, and she would drive them home.

Right before Jill started high school, her dad decided that they should move to the suburbs to get away from the Chicago gangs and drugs. But instead of protecting Jill from the destructive influence of urban decay, the move ended up introducing her to the teeming drug world of suburbia. One of the hallmarks of suburban teenage drug use was that—like Jill—the drug users were athletes, honor students, and student council members. Jill was very involved in school sports and continued to try to stay away from her chaotic home as much as she could. She was in school from 7 A.M. until 6:30 P.M.

The kids most like Jill were into LSD, cocaine, and any other drug that she wanted to try. Jill started hanging around kids who liked "tripping on acid" because she was curious about how these new drugs would make her feel. Presumably, she also wondered if it would make her home life easier to cope with than a couple cans of Schlitz.

"Drug use was just very prevalent in the suburbs, more than I had ever seen in Chicago," Jill remarked with hindsight. "After a football game, we would get a keg of beer and have a party at someone's house whose parents had left town, and my friends would start bringing out the drugs."

When Jill tried marijuana, she found it turned her into an extrovert, and from then on she smoked it every day. She would smoke and talk nonstop, feeling very confident. Just a few weeks after moving to this new high school, where she didn't fit in, the pot smoking provided her with an instant peer group.

Jill's new friends soon introduced her to the full panoply of drugs she could get at school: LSD, heroin, angel dust (PCP), amphetamines, and downers (sedatives). There was no limit to what she could buy at school and how much. Jill was so used to putting up a front that she continued to enjoy the reputation of being a good student. There was nothing to dislike about Jill; she was a straight A student who sat on the student council and was active in sports. Even as Jill got high in school more and more often, none of the teachers suspected anything. Jill was a brainy kid who could sit in class high as kite and still absorb everything the teacher said. She left her books in her locker, didn't study much, and still got As, so she would not in a million years have suspected that she had a problem. She bought the popular idea that drugs were great and that they expanded her mind.

Not only were Jill's smarts making it easier for her to conceal her habit, but she soon also figured out how to streamline her drug supply. She started selling drugs on campus for some of her schoolmates who were dealers. With her blond hair and good grades, she was perfect for the job because she didn't draw attention to herself and was never under suspicion. For every five "dimes" she sold, she would get to keep one for herself. This kept her supplied with a free stash of LSD, angel dust, pot, and heroin for her own use, and she was the most popular girl for anyone who wanted to get high.

During the summer after Jill turned 17, she started hanging out with a 30-something crowd who used intravenous drugs. To be helpful, she would shoot the stuff in their veins while they tightened the tourniquet. She had been taking care of her mom's diabetes for so long that she was as skilled as a regular nurse. She was fascinated by the way they toyed with death, but she drew the line at shooting up herself. This lasted until her dad found out she had been spending time with "these junkies" and beat her severely.

Jill had been walking a neighbor's dog that summer for pocket change. As she dropped the beagle off one day, she noticed stacks of money the guy was keeping in his home. She thought that if she could buy enough drugs she could go into business for herself, and maybe escape her violent father once and for all. Jill made sure the neighbor had left, and she came back at night. She pried a glass pane from the door without breaking it—she planned to put it back once the deed was done—and unlocked the door. While she was inside, the neighbor came back and saw the missing glass pane. He called the police and waited outside, making sure that the intruder remained in the house. Once the police arrived, Jill was taken to jail, where she sat until her dad picked her up later that night. He contained his rage until they were home. The beatings Jill continued to endure at home drove her back to drugs with a vengeance, which in turn put her in compromising positions, including a date rape and more beatings.

Jill eventually graduated from high school and decided that she wanted to become a nurse. After all, at nine she had started giving her mother insulin injections for her diabetes. Over the years, her mother's case had become increasingly complicated. Her heart started to fail, and she got venereal diseases from her husband, but Jill continued to be her nurse. Jill resuscitated her many times, and she knew all the paramedics in town on a first-name basis. Thanks to her outstanding grades, she was offered a complete scholarship to nursing school. The $20,000 would have paid the entire cost of getting a nursing degree, but her dad, who had only a sixth-grade education, equated the scholarship with welfare. His daughter did not need a handout.

"You're going to stay at home and take care of your mother," he announced as his final decision.

Faced with the prospect of being punched squarely in the face, all Jill could do was quietly fume over the double standard of being denied her own choices until she was 18, while being required to take on an adult caretaking role.

Jill finally turned 18 and enrolled in a nursing program. She went to the hospital stoned, not even doubting that she could get away with it. Being a nurse was a continuation of taking care of her ailing mother for years. She already knew most of the material, and she breezed through the first semester. It all seemed to go well until one day during the second semester, when her dad flew in a fit of rage and started throwing Jill into the wall and beating her. Jill was starting to feel more independent, being over 18 and halfway through nursing school. As far as she could remember, her dad never said that he was sorry after any of the beatings, and he never hugged her or showed love or affection. She looked at her swollen face in the bathroom mirror and decided she didn't have to take it anymore. She went into her mother's bedroom to tell her she was leaving home.

"You don't have to come back to take care of me," her mom said. "I am going to be all right."

They kissed good-bye. Jill packed a few clothes and her books, and closed the front door behind her. She never went back home.

Later that night her mother died of a heart attack. For the last 10 years, her heart had been attacked from within and from without, betrayed and bruised. Jill had done her best to mend her mother's heart back together year after year, but she needed to flee from the crushing home. Her mother escaped too, but through a different door.

If only I had been home, Jill kept thinking, I might have resuscitated her one more time. Years of anger welled up inside Jill, causing her to drop out of nursing school. To complicate things, Jill's boyfriend abandoned her after he got her pregnant. The abortion she had was a secret loss she had to bear alone, so Jill covered up her pain with increasing amounts of drugs and alcohol.

Jill married a man who proposed to her on their first date, and they had two children. Jill still drank and smoked pot, but not during the pregnancies, and she made good money at a local factory job. Under cover of her home, her drinking and drugging got worse. Her husband was an inveterate gambler who pawned Jill's wedding rings when she was pregnant with her second daughter.

"He gambled anything that wasn't nailed down," Jill said.

Jill came home one day to find a few dust bunnies on the floor where the waterbed had been. Like her mother, she kept hoping that her own husband would get better.

She left her first husband after a few years and met her second at a bar where she went to snort cocaine. He would start using coke a few hours before closing time, so he could sober up before they had to leave. To Jill, the fact that she never saw him drunk was admirable. That alone outweighed his pesky gambling habit. The biggest advantage was that she knew she could count on him to get her home when she was too drunk to drive.

Jill remembers sitting at the kitchen table while her husband was out gambling, looking at the booze and the pot on the table, and asking herself why she was so unhappy. She never thought it might be connected to the drugs, never realized that she might be happier if she was not stuck in a cycle of addiction. Cocaine precipitated Jill's fall and eventual realization. She would snort cocaine with friends after work, paying for it by selling marijuana to her coworkers. She brought the coke home, unable to stop, but she wanted to preserve the innocence of her daughters. Jill ordered them to stay in their rooms so they wouldn't find out. If they wanted to come out, they had to knock on the door, which gave Jill enough time to hide the mirrors, the cocaine, and the marijuana.

"Mom, can I come out?" one of her daughters would say, compliantly knocking on her bedroom door.

"Wait a minute!" Jill would say as she frantically tried to hide the drugs. "Wait a minute!" She straightened up the room in a panic.

"Mom! Can I please come out?" Her daughter would plead.

When Jill finally opened the door, her daughter stood crying in the middle of a puddle. Jill was heartbroken, but helpless to stop the cocaine use.

Things got instantly worse when Jill tried smoking crack. For the next six months, she sold marijuana and shoplifted from store after store to pay for her crack. She felt sick with guilt about taking her daughters with her on her drug excursions, leaving them in the car while she made deals, but the urge to get high outweighed any other consideration. Her credit cards were maxed out. At the height of her addiction, Jill's drug of choice was "whatever you had." She even got to the point of having sex with a drug dealer for a hit of crack.

Everybody at work knew Jill had a drug problem, but she was certain she was hiding it from everyone.

"I thought I was getting away with something," Jill explained to us. "You think you are fooling everybody, but in the end you are fooling only yourself."

On a night Jill had a fight with her husband, the police came and found marijuana she had left lying on the table. When they questioned her, Jill denied the pot was hers, so out of spite, her husband led the cops to a dusty mirror, a straw, and a razor blade. The cops ignored the cocaine paraphernalia, but they arrested Jill and her husband on felony possession of marijuana. While they sat in jail for two days, Jill's mother-in-law took care of the kids. Jill recalls the absurd phone conversation she had with her mother-in-law as she sat in jail on drug charges, denying she had a drug problem.

Jill's denial got her in more than one awkward situation. At a restaurant where she waitressed, she was joking around with a patron after he had told her he'd been clean and sober for six years.

"What meeting should I go to?" She asked jokingly. "AA, NA, CA?"

After a pause, the patron smiled and answered. "It doesn't matter, 'cause you could use them all."

The honesty hit her hard. Jill was offended and walked away in a huff.

Even the legal system seemed to validate her denial. During the year and a half of intensive probation she received for the drug possession, she was not drug-tested a single time, and she drank and smoked pot through the whole thing.

The first time Jill admitted she had a problem was when she received a DUI for driving home drunk after a nasty fight with her husband. Since she was still on probation, she decided to come clean with her probation officer about getting stoned throughout her probation period.

That first instance of honesty started a road to recovery for Jill, one that she would have liked to travel with her husband, whose gambling addiction was still untreated. But even as Jill checked herself into a detox program and worked on staying clean, trying again every time she relapsed, he continued drinking and gambling. Jill now had a sponsor, who began advising her to leave her husband. It was obvious that their respective roads were parting already.

Using drugs during relapses was getting more frustrating for Jill. Her emotional needs were starting to be met in healthier ways during the self-help groups she sporadically attended.

"One day," she told us, remembering a relapse. "I wanted to get more cocaine, and the beer wasn't good enough, and the marijuana wasn't good enough, and for some reason I found myself by my mother's grave, and I was scared to go home, and something told me to go into treatment."

Jill's sponsor got her a job washing dogs for less than minimum wage. Jill knew she would die if she kept using drugs, but she didn't want her kids to experience the loss of their mother. Her sponsor, who had been clean for over three years, kept saying that her husband was her next obstacle to recovery. The advice made sense to Jill; it was based on a level of self-respect she wished she had. Jill's husband had made it clear he would not change his ways. He sensed a change in Jill's attitude and faced her with a choice between him and her "fucking recovery."

What may seem like an easy choice, considering the terms, took some courage for Jill to utter: "My first priority has to be my recovery."

She wanted to have self-respect and also the respect of her children. Jill sat down with her four-year-old daughter to explain that they had to leave Dad—the other daughter was only 11 months old. She didn't know where they were going to stay, and she didn't have much money from washing dogs. Her daughter said it was OK, that God would take care of them.

The next guy Jill moved in with ended up verbally threatening her older daughter and hitting Jill. She immediately took her girls to a shelter, and for 11 months Jill's kids attended Al-a-tots meetings while she went to AA meetings. She had hoped that by staying clean, she would earn her husband's respect back and be part of a family again. By then, he told Jill he had met someone else and served her with divorce papers. The next day Jill went out and got drunk.

While living in the shelter, Jill attended self-help group meetings where she ran into Peter, whom she knew from treatment. Peter told Jill he knew of a place called Oxford House where she could stay. Jill was surprised to hear that there were 16 Oxford Houses in her area. She took her daughters to the house that had an opening, and they were accepted as members.

Jill still remembers how the daily "constructive confrontation" with the other women in the house forced her to face many issues that were central to the success of her recovery. Oxford House can help people with addictions at any stage of their recovery. Jill credits significant progress to the time she spent there. She admitted she was power-less several years before she came to live at the Oxford House, but after being in an emotionally abusive relationship for seven years, she needed help to recognize her codependent behavior. That's where the community of Oxford House helped her.

"I still struggle in the area of relationships," Jill admitted to us. "But in other areas I have really grown up."

New members have to conduct "one-on-ones," talks with house members during which they tell their stories. With every new house member they talk to, newcomers think of new ways to look at their stories, new insights.

"It's kind of like watching a play unfold," Jill remarked.

When asked if witnessing other people's pain could be depressing, Jill said it might put one in touch with one's own pain.

"There's something about going through some pain that helps you release it," Jill said. "You shouldn't be afraid of sharing anything," she adds about the support she experienced in the Oxford House com-munity.

Jill maintained, "They don't know how much they helped me. The ladies of my old house still call me and ask me to take them to a self-help group meeting. I still have keys to Oxford House, and when I'm not feeling good, I still go over to the house and grab somebody and have them listen to me. Or I will just show up to see what is going on, and I will be there for someone else. You are allowed to progress in your own recovery at your own pace. It's all about learning to clean up for yourself and taking care of yourself and financially taking care of yourself."

Once residents are ready to leave the community, they have already begun to generalize the Oxford House values, because they are so eas-ily applicable to the social contract outside.

"The older members are always showing the newcomers the bigger picture," Jill said.

After living in the Oxford House for four months, Jill moved to a transitional housing unit. But when she went there for her first night, she was so lonely that she called the Oxford House and began talk-ing to her friends. Because she was fearful of being on her own, she returned to the weekly business meetings, and she stayed involved with her friends in the Oxford House. Jill developed a home clean-ing business with flexible hours, so she was able to visit an Oxford

House, and help new residents get adjusted to the house or help with errands. Jill left the Oxford House in 1998, but she still stays close to the residents.

Jill is preparing to buy a house, but even though she is reaching this level of independence, she remains active in the Oxford House network, attending fundraising functions and chapter meetings. She hopes to one day be able to rent her own property to an Oxford House. This kind of lifelong commitment is the norm rather than the exception among Oxford House alumni. It is indicative of the quality of transformation alumni experience there. As Oxford House alumni like to say, "AA saved my life; Oxford House gave me a life."

After an initial period of resistance, residents often go the extra mile to clean up their lives. Jill remembered women who turned themselves in to clear up old police warrants. Others settled old financial debts or took parenting classes.

In keeping with the concept of harm reduction, acceptable addictions like cigarettes are allowed in some houses, but others limit cigarettes to a smoking room. Tolerance is an important value at Oxford House, and cultural variations are respected as long as the culture of recovery is respected.

Responsibility is also encouraged by awarding house positions to residents who show progress. Not long after she moved in, Jill was asked to become an officer, and each position offered her a new way to take responsibility. Jill learned that she didn't need a man to gain self-respect, that she could have the camaraderie of women and feel just as good. Through the mutual relationships in her house, she helped women who were newer to sobriety, sometimes staying up all night talking. She also got support from her roommates when she ran into problems. Most importantly, she could always count on them to understand the issues unique to recovery from addiction.

Jill still gets a kick out the incongruity of making a "dope fiend" responsible for writing checks. It is not just useful for someone to learn how to write a check for the first time in her or his life, but it is also satisfying for that person to know that sound fiscal practice has earned the house enough cash to buy a big-screen TV. Oxford House alumni all agree that those responsibilities make them more employable. The comptroller insures that all the rents (around $70 to $80 a week per person) and fines are paid to the treasurer, who in turn writes checks, but only during mandatory business meetings, in front of everyone. The treasurer leaves the signing of house checks to another resident, often the president. The community keeps the positions of house president, treasurer, comptroller, and secretary accountable simply by being part of every action they take. The transparency of all the transactions ensures that fraud is unlikely. All community members share the power of each house position. Financial loss to a house can occur when a resident falls behind on rent and leaves due to a relapse or is unable to find work, but interventions like putting a resident on a financial contract can prevent emerging situations from degenerating.

Alumni agree the structure of everyday life at Oxford House is at the heart of its success. Fines are levied on residents for a variety of violations, beginning at $5 for leaving a dish in the sink. Fines are deposited in the house checking account, along with the weekly rents, and used for upgrades to the home. The autonomy of each house allows for variations in fines. Some will fine a resident for leaving a cigarette in the ashtray, others won't. New residents quickly learn the rules of their house. Some houses fine $50 for leaving lint in the clothes dryer. The only $50 fines in the Northern Lake County Oxford Houses are for smoking in bed—for obvious safety reasons—and not answering call waiting, which could be signaling a distress call.

"I got fined $40 the first week I lived there," Jill said. "You have to be responsible."

Contracts can be drafted between the house and residents who don't pay their bills or whose behavior is problematic. Financial and behavior contracts are enforced by the community and include a loss of privileges for the duration of the contract. This way, the community is able to confront the biggest stumbling block new residents encounter: being able to recognize their own behavior. Lacking the self-consciousness to see themselves acting in problematic ways, new residents are forced by the community to face and eventually accept what everyone else can plainly see. Once in a while, newcomers who are especially stubborn in their refusal to change are put on the "grow or go" contract. Under this last-resort contract, they have to live out of a cardboard box in which all their belongings are kept. The box is a symbol of their precarious position. If they persist in the problematic behavior, they are immediately evicted and have to leave the house carrying their cardboard box.

Because of the pervasive nature of addiction, rules reach far into the personal lives of residents. Honesty must characterize all relationships, even romantic ones, so monogamy is the rule. Residents would not allow one of their own to be romantically involved with more than one person, and they enforce this by allowing only one special guest to enter the resident's bedroom. The relative loss of privacy is quickly accepted by new residents as the price for regaining a sense of responsibility.

"We do have independence in an Oxford House, though," Jill explained to us. "You do not have to tell people where you are going or what you are doing, unless you are doing an overnight outside the house."

Running the house like a business may seem to contradict the organic, unregimented nature of the community spirit, but the rules and their enforcement through fines and contracts help to guarantee that the social support network will always be there for residents. Fines are often used to buy upgrades for the home—a men's house was able to buy new blinds—so people who paid the fines end up benefiting from upgrades along with their community. A woman who had paid substantial fines talked the house into buying a barbecue they needed, and ended up looking at the fines she paid as positives. Sometimes, though, residents know when to make exceptions to the businesslike attitude. Even though the house president is supposed to have her own room, it usually ends up going to a woman with a child.

"That's when the house is run less like a business, and people show some heart," Jill said.

Oxford Houses also constitute a larger community that can be witnessed in more than the monthly chapter meeting. Residents from one house have been known to paint another house or do a variety of maintenance jobs. Residents with certain skills, like plumbing, frequently help out other houses when they have a need for this type of service. Several members have also gone to fellow houses, urging residents to register to vote, thereby helping formerly disenfranchised citizens back into the political process.

Residents who move in with children pay a slightly higher rent and are also held responsible for their children's behavior. A single parent who lives at an Oxford House with a child is given some latitude in parenting style, but no abuse is tolerated, which is more than can be said of the community at large. Parents can be fined if they fail to clean up after their children, or if they don't spend enough time parenting.

No restrictions are placed on children, other than obvious safety constraints, but children are often frightened at first by their new living situation. Very young children have difficulty sharing their space with so many strangers, even though women with children usually

get their own rooms. Jill related her amazement at the positive change
in children's attitude once they accept their extended family. Mothers
also benefit from the expanded concept of family, when residents offer
them a few hours of rest by babysitting their children. Regular homes
don't have a pool of babysitters permanently in the house. Children
are effectively raised by all the women in the house (there are also a
few houses for single male parents). The relief for the natural mother
is significant, but other women who may have lost custody of children
before they became sober also enjoy being able to mother a child. Jill,
whose children are older, also enjoys being around younger children.
Men like Bob also have a chance to practice their fathering skills with
the children who run around the yard during chapter meetings.

Jill—who had always seemed to get along better with men—noticed
that it was especially challenging for her to live with other women.

"Women hold on to stuff," Jill noted. "They get very defensive and
very emotional."

A significant amount of healthy competition between men and
women drives Oxford Houses to outdo each other. Jill acknowledged
that women—because of the way they are socialized—tended to isolate less than men. Consequently, she said, women tended to naturally
meet the socialization goal at every Oxford House, whereas men
tended to isolate more. Jill also noticed that men tended to compen-
sate for this by keeping busy doing house chores.

"Men don't socialize as much, so their general living area is often
kept neater," Jill said.

Cooking is not one of the house chores, and residents are responsible for their own cooking, but women's and men's houses often pride
themselves on holding unity dinners, communal meals voluntarily
cooked by residents. The sharing of food is entirely up to residents.

House chores are divided by assigning each resident a room, and
cleanliness is graded each time the chore is supposed to be done.

The sense of responsibility and accountability to the community at
Oxford House is no different than the social contract one encounters
outside, but it is enforced more consistently. The behavior contract
works better inside this healing community than in the surrounding
society because of the lack of anonymity inside an Oxford House. The
community of an Oxford House knows what all of its members do, so
that honesty becomes the easiest value to govern one's life.

"If you're up at four in the morning, and a resident walks in, looking like she's been using, you have to wake up the whole house for an
emergency meeting," Jill explained.

Jill told the story of a woman in her house who was known to be a diabetic (the entrance interview includes this type of information) and who started eating all the food. Residents recognized this as a sign that something was bothering her. After being confronted by community members, the woman started talking about her problem and stopped abusing her body.

Mutuality in the relationships of Oxford House members allows movement to take place naturally. Recovery happens as a by-product of a healthy environment, a sanctuary guarded by limits members set on each other. No one could individually claim credit for the group's success, just like no one could be blamed for individual relapses. The welfare of each is insured by the group, and the group's fate relies on each member. Despite Bob's humble qualifier that he was only doing what he should have been doing all along, recovery from drug and alcohol addiction is always a wondrous thing. What makes it so awe-inspiring at Oxford House is that it reveals itself as a natural healing process that occurs when it is allowed to. This natural process can be credited in part to the normalizing nature of Oxford House. Its traditions and values have created a healthy environment without falling into the utopian trap where some communes have disappeared. Oxford Houses are discreetly integrated into the world around them and hard to notice because the structures that define them are internal rather than external. They are a superb example of healthy, courageous living in an interconnected world, in spite of adversity.

Chapter Meetings: Democracy in Action

The simple, healing tasks of everyday life in the Oxford House community are held in a place of honor during one of the chapter meetings that occur monthly on Saturday evenings. Representatives for 7 to 10 houses converge during these meetings. The willingness to devote a Saturday evening to the Oxford House cause conveys the deep level of investment those in attendance have toward the community.

One such meeting took place at an Oxford House in Waukegan, Illinois, a small city north of Chicago. The unassuming frame house looked like all the others on the quiet residential street, with painted wood siding and a quaint, slightly antique feel. A sign on the front door directed visitors to walk down the alley to the back of the house.

In the postage-stamp backyard, wedged between the house and the garage, a crowd of 50 sat quietly in rows of folding chairs listening to a panel of 7 or 8. These men and women were almost entirely in their forties and fifties—old-timers in the shortened life span of the average drug abuser. As the residents huddled together to reminisce and talk about their everyday concerns, their faces told a hundred stories with the same ending: Oxford House helped me learn how to live.

A few new residents glanced around nervously, looking a little disoriented. Older residents had an air of self-confidence and physical well-being. Children ran around playing and cicadas hummed in two huge maples arched over a painted back porch, where more people ate chicken and watermelon from paper plates.

Peter was in the middle of a discussion with an animated woman sitting in the crowd. The woman, in her thirties, was wire-thin. With a slightly defiant tone, she reported having been fined by the Oxford House she shared with six other women because she had repeatedly disregarded the 15-minute phone limit.

"If someone overuses something in the house, everyone has to pitch in to cover," Peter reminded the crowd. "The phone bill doesn't lie."

Peter explained that Oxford House residents paid for their phone usage on the honor system, circling their calls on the posted phone bill. Discrepancies were looked at amicably at first, but when repeated violations of house rules threatened to destabilize the fragile communal economy, they were dealt with diligently.

The woman was resistant to the greater good of the commune, unable to get past her selfish interest. It was causing some chaos in the meeting, but people continued to patiently explain the rules to her. Susan, who was leaning on the porch railing overlooking the backyard, raised her hand.

"Hi! My name is Susan, and I'm an addict," Susan said.

"Hi, Susan!" The crowd chanted.

"Are we supposed to monitor each other's phone time?" Susan continued. "I mean, what am I supposed to do if she is having a fight with her man? Am I going to hover over her, or what?"

As the crowd tensely weighed the pros and cons of Susan's suggestion, a graying man tried to diffuse the situation with a humorous comment.

"If you're fighting for hours with your old man, maybe it's time to get yourself a new old man!" he said, sending waves of laughter through the crowd.

Peter agreed with Susan that there could be no spying on one another, but when a man sitting in the front row said that this was an especially bad problem in women's Oxford Houses, Peter was quick to nip the sexist remark in the bud.

"Men have this problem too. What is damaging is when someone has an ongoing problem and the rest of the house is covering it up. The covering up is what needs to be looked at. It's codependent behavior," Peter continued. "All of us have problems with being codependent."

Someone on the panel moved the agenda to the next house, and a man hesitantly recited a report listing the number of beds in the house, vacant beds, the house bank account balance, and whether all house utility bills were current. The man kept checking with his neighbor, who nodded encouragingly and whispered to him what to do next, and he continued his house report. He had recently been promoted into the house treasurer position, and he was still getting used to the new responsibility. With eyes wide open and eyebrows raised, the man was obviously surprising himself with his new treasurer function, as he proudly passed forward a check for Oxford House chapter dues and another check for fundraising tickets sold that month. Finally, the man reported on house unity—the overall communal integrity of the house—and on the one drug and alcohol relapse in the house for that month. In this case, one man was evicted from the house for hiding prescription medication in his room and drinking alcohol, a serious violation of the contract residents sign upon moving in. An eviction does not necessarily ban a resident for life, but it is usually a required action to protect the rest of the residents. As a resident reminded everyone, "One or two bad apples can spoil the whole bunch."

This particular eviction had been carried out in a less-than-perfect way, so it required further discussion. When residents in that particular house realized that one of them was using drugs and alcohol, they should have called an emergency house meeting right away, but for some reason some time went by before anyone did anything.

"If you keep quiet when you find out a resident is using, you might as well be using too," Peter explained. It underscored the constant need to minimize chaos in communal life. Because this was a monthly chapter meeting, several houses were getting the benefit of the learning experience.

Susan raised her hand to speak again. "Hi! My name is Susan, and I'm an addict," she said again.

"Hi, Susan!" The crowd answered as warmly as the first time.

"When you cover up something, it's dangerous for the sanctity of the house," Susan said.

By stressing the word *sanctity*, Susan credited the success of this healing community on its ability to preserve sacredness in everyday life. Even in the most restrictive, profane sense of the word, she placed the welfare of the group before her own comfort. This was at the heart of the Oxford House success.

Most Oxford House residents took Susan's use of the word *sanctity* in a deep, spiritual sense.

As Joe pointed out, "Addiction is the loss of your spirituality, and once you get that back there's nothing that you couldn't do."

Joe had moved into an Oxford House six months earlier. A drug relapse after three years of sobriety suggested that Joe needed something more than treatment. Joe needed the safety of the Oxford House environment to achieve the attitude shift. He understood the reason for his relapse to be his character defects—his inability to deal constructively with life's frustrations—and he needed the supportive environment of Oxford House until he learned to cope in a more healthy way.

Joe described recovery at Oxford House as "definitely a quest for spirituality. Once we get to a certain level of spirituality, and only then are we ready to venture out on our own."

For Joe, this quest for the spiritual was made up of the helping relationships that form every time Oxford House residents give each other advice, support, or feedback. Those relationships were in fact the essence of sacredness for Joe. Everyone, regardless of seniority, could constructively remind another resident of responsibilities and expectations. Helping relationships were also constantly evolving in the more benign realm of daily interaction. As Joe explained, people moved into Oxford Houses to ward off isolation and confront their relational deficiencies in the safe and sacred space of the house. By putting themselves in a situation where healthy relating was unavoidable, residents put their own behavior in front of the objective eye of others. By the same token, they themselves could see the behavior of others with objectivity.

"If you isolate, you'll continue doing the same thing that you've always done," Joe said. "You can't see what you're doing from the inside, but others can see what you are up to from the outside."

Gradually, residents raise each other's consciousness about the pernicious influence addiction had in their lives, and they use their understanding of which stimuli caused them to relapse to stay away from the wrong people, places, or things.

In return for keeping the greater good in mind, residents receive rewards, which could consist of being trusted with a house position like treasurer. For someone who had never had a checking account, being invested with the responsibility of writing checks to pay house bills is a great source of pride.

Self-centered, selfish types don't do well at Oxford House.

As Joe noted, "In my house, there are eight, so I have seven other people to think about."

This creates an opportunity for residents to practice a greater flexibility of the self, which in turn increases their coping abilities. Joe has grown concerned for the welfare of others in the house.

"I won't allow myself to be selfish," he said, "because it's just not fair to others." Joe's move from destructive self-centeredness to empathy and care toward fellow humans is emblematic of the profound success these types of communities can bring about in the lives of drug addicts and alcoholics.

Success at any of the 36 Oxford Houses spread out across Illinois (there are over 1,000 nationwide) is not defined in the same way as it is in the surrounding culture. Residents share only a few of the trappings of material wealth that define success in the American consumer culture. Oxford House residents view themselves as wealthy if they live sober lives according to values of honesty, responsibility, and self-transcendence.

The choice Oxford House residents make to live communally instead of following the pursuit of self-interested individualism with the rest of America is one obstacle to Oxford Houses being accepted more widely. People in the neighborhoods where Oxford Houses are established are not the problems. Landlords, who are not known for being fond of drunks and drug addicts, love to rent to Oxford House residents, because they must have jobs (according to house rules), pay rent, and take good care of the property. Residents who receive disability payments and choose not to work must be enrolled in school at least part-time or do volunteer work. Residents can be self-employed, but they must pay an additional fee to the house if they use it as a home office. Most neighbors are won over by the high level of responsibility they witness next door. In fact, with their automatic eviction rule for relapses, Oxford House residents may well be the most responsible ones on the block. The occasional perception of Oxford House residents and addicts in general as marginal elements of society overlooks the important lessons they can share with their neighbors, many of whom may be invisible, functional addicts to drugs, alcohol, television, Internet porn, consumer goods, or work. It would be ironic if those who learned healthy values through costly mistakes were seen as destabilizing elements of a community, when they are the ones who are proving day after day that unselfish, healthy communal life is possible regardless of material wealth.

Bob thought that the public at large could also learn a few things from the way people live at Oxford Houses, because addiction was a model that could explain social problems on a larger scale, not just in terms of individuals who use drugs. A psychologist named Ralph Metzner argued very similar ideas.

Metzner (1992) used psychiatric terminology to describe social ills—terms that are usually reserved to diagnose individuals. For example, people's inability to stop destroying their natural environment is like an addiction. Indeed, the destruction continues even though the obvious consequence is the end of human life. Metzner traces this kind of global suicide back to a human superiority complex over the rest of creation—in other words, we feel like everything is ours for the taking, and we have dibs on it. It is as though we were all struck with collective amnesia; we forgot our old ways of looking at the natural world with humility and with respect for its infinite complexity.

By virtue of his experience as a recovering heroin addict, Bob had reached the same advanced insights as a transpersonal psychologist. Once people could get past their preconceptions, they might indeed learn a few things from life at Oxford House. Neighborhoods for Oxford Houses have to be safe and close to schools (for women's houses), public transportation, stores, and businesses. When an Oxford House is opened, a recovery home coordinator meets with neighbors to introduce the idea. Protests are rare, but the former mayor of a town north of Chicago led picketing against an Oxford House that was scheduled to open on his block. The house was protected under the Fair Housing Act for people with disabilities, but ended up selecting another neighborhood. Oxford Houses give high priority to friendly neighbor relations.

Historically, the strongest objections to the Oxford House system came from traditional treatment clinicians. When Paul Molloy founded the first house, people who worked in treatment centers made anonymous calls and sent in the fire marshals. They could not stomach that addicts could recover by themselves, without the clinicians' eminent authority.

Time after time, Oxford House residents and alumni tell a slightly different version of their success. When Greg told his story, he seemed to place particular importance on the way he was treated with dignity.

"Here I was, an addict." Greg explained. "I stole, I hurt people all my life, and the first thing they do when I get to Oxford House is give me a key! And a few weeks later, they give me a checkbook, and ask me to be the treasurer!"

Greg was deeply moved by the repeated gestures of trust, an emotion he credits with restoring his own hope.

CHAPTER 3

The Dignity of Aging

Our nation's aging population will surge as baby boomers enter their senior years. The 12 percent of the population that is now 65 years or older will increase to 21 percent by 2030 (Harper, 1995). Unfortunately, those who retire often face loss of income, loss of contacts with associates, and loss of jobs. Among those who have retired, over 1.7 million elderly persons live in nursing homes or similar residential facilities (Levine & Perkins, 1997). Medicaid covers 70 percent of nursing home residents, but it only pays an average of $105 a day, which barely covers the costs of housing, food, prescription drugs, therapy, nurses, and other employees.

Whereas the average nursing home costs nearly $4,000 a month, assisted-living residences, for which residents must pay out of pocket, cost about $1,800 a month. There are about 10,000 of these facilities, and they house nearly 800,000 elderly Americans. Most assisted-living centers do not have full-time nurses on staff, but residents actually receive more medication than patients in nursing homes. Unfortunately, the care provided in many nursing homes and assisted-living centers is exceedingly poor, and there are widespread allegations of substandard care, neglect, and even preventable death.

In order to create an alternative, Michael and Lilo Salmon founded Housing Opportunities and Maintenance for the Elderly (H.O.M.E.) in 1982 as an organization committed to creating familylike housing, as well as moving and furnishing services for low-income elders in Chicago. Before founding this organization, Michael and Lilo had worked with elderly people for many years. Lilo described most senior housing projects as "ghettos for old people" (Anderson, 1999). Michael realized during this early work that the elderly severely lacked funds for housing, not to mention for medication and food.

When Nathalie Salmon, Michael and Lilo's only child, was killed in a traffic accident at age 15, Lilo poured her energy into H.O.M.E. Helping the elderly helped keep Lilo "from going insane." The mission of H.O.M.E. was to treat elderly people with respect, to preserve their dignity and independence, and to consider them friends rather than clients. Lilo, a social worker, believed that the housing problems of the elderly could be addressed more effectively by creating intergenerational communities, homes where all age groups were represented.

When Lilo and Michael opened the Pat Crowley House in 1983 and the Oak Park House in 1985, they wanted to create places where people could be treated with respect, tolerance, and love, like grandparents would hope to be treated by grandchildren. (The Oak Park House was closed in 1995, mostly because H.O.M.E. did not own the building, and the residents were moved to other H.O.M.E. residences.) To this end, their intergenerational homes were established not as agency programs administered by professionals, but as communities where staff members lived. The Pat Crowley Housed 12 elderly individuals, a full-time coordinator and family, and several college students who received free room and board in exchange for completing chores. In addition to its elderly residents, the Oak Park House housed student volunteers. The rest of the Oak Park House staff lived at the Nathalie Salmon House. Lilo and Michael wanted to create a setting that made life worthwhile, where the staff members lived and were part of the community. These intergenerational homes offered elderly residents "an alternative to high rents, loneliness, isolation and the burden of day-to-day self care" and "an innovative communal possibility for a new and different lifestyle that fosters companionship and friendship by offering the residents the opportunity of caring for each other" (H.O.M.E., 1991, p. 8). When asked how she was able to create such a warm environment, Lilo said, "I don't create anything. It's love…it's all built on simplicity… and common sense" (McMahon & Pontari, 1993).

In an article for the Chicago *Reader*, Guthrie (1999) described the Pat Crowley House as a "three-flat in Rogers Park with private bedrooms for low-income seniors who have lost their homes. The house has table tennis and a pool table in the basement, a sitting room, porch swings on each floor, intercoms in each hall and bedroom, and a garden teeming with flowers and bird feeders."

Erikson (1959) described the journey into old age as a final stage of life focusing on integrity versus despair. Integrity connotes acceptance of mortality and the human life cycle. This last part of life deals with making peace with one's mortality, finding meaning in one's life, and finding the sacred within everyday experiences. Often, individuals who lack support or live in poor conditions don't get a chance to experience old age with grace, unless they are as fortunate as the people we talked to. These are their stories.

Trudy's Story

"Society just wanted to throw me away," Trudy said. "I was practically dead. They wanted to stick me somewhere so I wouldn't die in the street and someone would get blamed for it. Seniors with bad health are totally isolated, and nobody cares once the insurance has run out."

At 80, Trudy outlived everyone in her family. Her husband was long gone, and her daughter had been dead for a year. Trudy was born and raised in Michigan, then lived in Chicago for the next 60 years. She held several jobs in advertising, product sales, and banking. She had fond memories of these positions and of the relative independence they afforded her.

About 15 years into retirement, Trudy still kept busy. Thanks to her accounting background, she got part-time work in dress shops and offices. When Trudy was not at work and needed company, she just got on a bus headed to the mall.

"I would go out and sit on benches by the bus stop and talk to people while they were waiting for a bus."

Her work routine was interrupted by a case of bronchial pneumonia that required a couple of days in the hospital. During treatment for the pneumonia, tests revealed cancer. The hospital stay stretched to over three months. The hospital staff constantly reminded Trudy that her insurance would run out when radiation treatment ended, and they moved her to a rehabilitation unit and nursing facility, where she stayed for five weeks.

Trudy found her stay at the nursing facility to be an embittering and depressing experience. It was bad enough to have cancer, but there was the additional trauma and injustice of her insurance running out once her radiation treatment ended. Then there were small things that scared Trudy. There was no phone in Trudy's room, so she had to use the facility's single pay phone when she needed to contact the outside world. For the moment, she had a single room, paid for by her insurance, but she was told she would have to share a room with two other patients once her coverage ran out. The nursing facility explained that, in order to stay there at all, Trudy would have to sign over her monthly Social Security check. For Trudy, who had been raised among charitable folks, this abandonment could have been enough to become a cynic, but Trudy did what she could to turn negative thoughts into something constructive. She stared at the chrome and blue vinyl wheelchair they gave her when she arrived at the nursing home. It was like they were encouraging her to get sicker and die. She needed to exercise, so she pushed the empty wheelchair around the nursing home like a shopping cart. Other residents cheered her on as she went by, complimenting her on her ingenuity. Trudy wasn't fishing for compliments; she was only trying to move her legs and find something to do. Trudy's little excursions through the nursing home had another, less desirable effect: she saw more human suffering and hopelessness than she could bear. Many people were a lot worse off than she was. Most in the cafeteria could not eat on their own. They waited for a nurse to shove a spoonful of puree into their mouth, while spilled food collected on the front of their gowns. On the one hand, she was glad she could still take care of her own basic needs, but she also realized that she was looking at her own future, and that was too horrible to contemplate.

The most depressing thought for Trudy was that so many people would feel that a nursing home was their only choice. Where were their families? How could no one in this supposedly civilized world have thought of a better system than the deathly triangle of an empty apartment, a hospital bed, and a nursing home?

For the next two years, Trudy had three more operations to remove other tumors. After these short hospital stays, she had to recuperate at home alone. She had trouble getting around to feed herself, much less to do the needed house chores, and she couldn't go outside. She got on the phone and called a friend, but no amount of commiseration seemed to help. Alone and unsure of how to survive with her ailments, Trudy was feeling desperate. The building elevator worked only part of the time, and when it was out of order, Trudy had to drag her laundry down to the basement. It was easier just to stay up there. She wondered how long it would take before anyone noticed she was gone if something happened to her. Trudy mentioned how much she suffered from isolation to a social worker, who arranged a meeting with Caren from H.O.M.E.

Around the time Caren first met with Trudy, most of the elderly served by H.O.M.E. lived on $530 a month, a near impossibility in modern urban environments. Most seniors spent around 70 percent of their income on rent for an apartment that did not usually suit their needs. That did not leave much money for food and medication. H.O.M.E. provided free help in finding government-subsidized apartments, free moving, and free furniture. When elderly renters were in danger of being evicted, H.O.M.E. helped them find housing that was more affordable and provided them with all the furniture in the new rental places. In addition, H.O.M.E. volunteers repainted the apartments and installed all the donated furniture for free before seniors moved into their new, cheaper places. The elderly recipients of this help were often moved to tears when the crews declined to accept their tips and they realized that all the crew members wanted was to help them. That left more money for seniors to buy food and medication. Still, inadequate urban planning left many seniors stranded far away from convenient and affordable commercial centers, so H.O.M.E. provided a free shopping bus to drive seniors to shopping centers where they could stretch their meager resources. It should be noted that a mall located a block away could be inaccessible to many elderly people. Finally, and this was the most appealing feature to Trudy, H.O.M.E. offered intergenerational shared living in a six-flat building, the Pat Crowley House, purchased in 1983, and a newer and larger building, the Nathalie Salmon House.

The Pat Crowley House was home to 12 seniors, 4 students, and a young couple (Caren and her husband) with their 2 children. Every month, in exchange for rent, meals, utilities, and house-provided services, residents paid 80 percent of their income or $791, whichever was less. With the remainder, they paid for personal items, clothing, prescriptions, and doctor bills, but a student nursing program from Loyola provided a student nurse to check on their vitals once a week. Other volunteer professionals—chiropractors, podiatrists, and ophthalmologists—also came in to help out, and volunteered their services to residents.

As she listened to Caren's description of the H.O.M.E. organization, Trudy felt her eyes welling up. It had none of the scary aspects of the medical facilities, yet it provided the care she needed most. As fat tears rolled down her face, she knew this was a place for her, but it was difficult to accept that she was one of the less fortunate, those in need of help.

"I'm not dead yet," Trudy said. "Please! I've got feelings."

Gradually, Trudy accepted that she was in need of others' charity. She was first invited to have lunch at the Pat Crowley House. She loved the roomy vintage house and the feeling of conviviality at the table. Trudy moved in a few weeks later, after all her paperwork was in place (background and credit check, doctor's letter, and landlord reference). At first, she could not believe that she had free reign on her nights and days. The nursing home had been so restrictive, with all the rules, and the apartment so confining, that this level of freedom took some getting used to. She could go into the kitchen in the middle of night to fill her water bottle if she wanted to. For several weeks, Trudy had to remind herself that she could do as she pleased. Trudy could leave the house to go out at her leisure, even to stay somewhere else overnight. As long as H.O.M.E. residents told someone that they were going somewhere and how long they would be gone, they were free to go anytime.

With no formal visiting hours or regimented rules, residents knew that their friends and relatives were welcome anytime to visit or to stay for a meal. As soon as Caren explained these community rules to new residents, they knew that she actually cared about them. To many, this warm welcome was in sharp contrast to experiences they had in nursing homes that enforced much stricter rules. Because of liability, these nursing homes needed to know where their residents were at all times. As a community, H.O.M.E. residents were much closer to a family, and were therefore much less concerned with getting sued. Family being the natural way humans grouped themselves and related to each other, people at H.O.M.E. were better able to create their own friendships and their own relationships. The lack of a controlling influence from staff let natural relational phenomena happen more organically; it was probably the single most important factor in fighting alienation in this elderly population.

By far the most pleasant surprise for Trudy was that she did not have to sign over her monthly Social Security check to H.O.M.E. staff. All the assisted-living communities on the photocopied list the caseworker had given her required such financial surrender as a condition of admission. They controlled the finances of their residents and doled out allowances to them, between $30 and $90 a month, like parents did with their kids. Trudy would pay rent at the Pat Crowley

House, and as far as she was concerned, that was the biggest freedom of all.

Caren and other H.O.M.E. staff members also provided opportunities for residents to relate during outings to restaurants, concerts, plays, gardens, museums, and the zoo. Preplanned gatherings were usually centered around holidays and the biweekly community nights. All the residents who had birthdays were celebrated in a monthly party. On Christmas and New Year's Eve, Caren got together with all the residents, her husband, and her kids to toast the occasion with a glass of champagne. They served snacks and hors d'oeuvres, and exchanged presents. Thanksgiving was usually a memorable meal. Neighbors were invited to the summer family picnic. The Nathalie Salmon House joined in for an occasional backyard party.

These scheduled activities at first seemed similar to those offered in less welcoming institutional settings, but the optional attendance at H.O.M.E. left residents with the initiative and the control of their own lives. For example, the more able decided to help those in wheelchairs and, through these actions, made community self-evident. This way, the infantilizing treatment of residents that was so pervasive and disempowering in most institutional settings for the elderly was not an issue at H.O.M.E.

Another concrete reminder that dignity of H.O.M.E. residents was preserved was the privacy of their own room to keep their personal possessions. Nursing homes usually provided patients with curtain partitions, Caren said.

When Trudy noted that the furniture was not covered with transparent plastic covers as she had seen in the nursing home, Caren the house manager chuckled.

"Of course," Caren said. "This is where we live. We eat here, we drop crumbs, and we spill things. This is your home now."

That comment helped Trudy to realize fully that this was a place where people really cared about her. She felt delivered from the nursing home and the hospital.

It quickly became obvious to Trudy that her isolation had not been a matter of choice, but of environment. Now that she had the full run of a place she shared with 10 other elderly men and women, she spent very little time in her room, unless she went in there to sleep or to make her bed. Those who had their own televisions occasionally retired to their rooms to watch their favorite shows alone, but Trudy preferred to watch TV with others in the living room.

Like the majority of elderly people, Trudy had suffered numerous losses by the time she reached the age of 80. Loved ones died in waves. One left, then another did too, before she could properly mourn the first one. Unprocessed grief and its accompanying sense of vulnerability set in, creating the need for a uniquely supportive environment. The fact that these emotional needs were usually compounded by declining health made nursing homes seem woefully inadequate. As Trudy remarked, nursing home environments seemed to be sending residents a not-so-subliminal message that they should just die. By comparison, the symbolism that emanated from H.O.M.E. environments was one of positive and hopeful dignity.

Caren described "a vast difference between the nursing home experience and H.O.M.E." She said nursing homes generally housed one to four people in a room with a bed, a nightstand, a mirror on a dresser door, and only part of an already small closet. Sitting rooms, she said, were basically for show, not for people to actually use. TV rooms were also set up in impractical, uninviting ways, without any attempt to approach the comfort one would expect in a regular home. At H.O.M.E., the living room looked just like the one used by the average American family, down to the armrest doily and crocheted afghan. People at nursing homes worked in shifts (7 A.M. to 3 P.M., 3 P.M. to 11 P.M., and 11 P.M. to 7 A.M.) that contributed to an institutional and mechanistic atmosphere. Instead of feeling like they were at home, nursing home residents feel like they are in a factory, a system. Nursing home staff care for residents with a certain amount of distance and objectivity, as required by their professional stance. On the contrary, H.O.M.E. staff have the engrossment necessary for a successful subjective approach to caring, because their workplace is also their own home. The latter approach helps to prevent treating elderly people like objects or problems to be solved. Instead, H.O.M.E. residents are seen as human beings first, and are treated as such, with love, respect, and dignity.

While they reserved subjective qualities for the treatment of residents, H.O.M.E. managers regarded their finances very objectively. Financially speaking, H.O.M.E. allocated resources in a more responsible manner than most institutions: 90 percent of all the money raised went to direct service.

Everyone ate lunch and dinner together on two large tables in the dining room, also where H.O.M.E. residents played games and chatted. Trudy was pleasantly surprised by the quality of the lovingly prepared meals. In the morning, Trudy was free to get up when she felt like it, and to eat what she wanted for breakfast. Some days, it was a piece of toast and a glass of juice; on other days she had a big bowl of cereal. Lunches were often pretty lively, with residents talking back and forth between the two tables, trying to swipe each other's desserts, and generally enjoying each other's company. Patch, a short beagle, arrived in the house with Caren and her family in 1996 as a gift to Caren's daughter, and also as a gift to all. He patrolled the room for any scraps that might fall off the table. Patch was more than a mascot to the residents, who joked that he was the real owner of the house. Strutting around very independently, Patch generally wouldn't let anyone pick him up, but he was known to jump up on a couch or a bed to snuggle with H.O.M.E. residents. He also let residents know when the telephone or the doorbell was ringing.

"We all belong to him," Trudy said.

The four college students who also lived in the Pat Crowley House did the cooking on weekends and got things from the top shelves that residents couldn't reach or from the basement storage. Students invited Trudy and other residents to join in creative weekend activities (arts and crafts, cards, games, and bingo), and also helped by picking out good films at the video store. Activities were held regularly at the house, but residents participated voluntarily. For residents who disliked the predictability of an activity schedule (it can be reminiscent of a nursing home), the freedom of H.O.M.E. allowed spontaneity. Sometimes, residents all got together on the spur of the moment and made cupcakes. A key theme at H.O.M.E. was that every senior deserved to live in a genuine community. The H.O.M.E. Annual Report (H.O.M.E., 2000) described how this was achieved: "Our volunteers prepare meals, deliver food, run errands, and sort donated items. They become friends by simply holding a hand and visiting. We have an artist who provides arts and craft classes to our residents, and we have another volunteer who gives massages."

Trudy was still poor and sick, but not alone.

Myron's Story

Like Trudy's, Myron's life had been largely about separation and solitude. After a divorce from a childless marriage and four years of retirement, he found himself in sparse company. Myron had lived in the same place for 25 years. Many of his former friends had died or moved away. When a stroke landed Myron in a nursing home, he knew that he felt lonely and scared, but he could not think of a solution.

In 1934, young Myron learned to play bass violin in the high school orchestra, a skill he used to make some money playing restaurants and supper clubs. After attending piano-tuning school in Chicago, he got a job with the Wurlitzer Piano Company. For 20 years, he tuned Wurlitzer pianos during the week and performed on weekend nights in downtown Chicago nightclubs and suburban country clubs. Myron was occasionally asked to replace an absent musician in an out-of-town band and soon found himself playing for new performers, like Jimmy Durante and Bob Crosby (Bing's brother).

Myron developed bursitis from carrying the instrument around on one shoulder. Cortisone shots alleviated the pain for three months, until the other shoulder also gave out, ending Myron's budding career as a musician. The piano-tuning work stopped about five years later, at which time Myron retired.

After his divorce, Myron had grown accustomed to living alone. He was content with the superficial human contact he got at work. For the last 20 years, the colleagues with whom he had shared long hours were sufficient company. Retirement couldn't be that different, he thought. As it turned out, he didn't really miss his colleagues for the first few months. He enjoyed taking walks around the block for exercise and watching TV in his velour recliner, but after a while, that changed. Myron started to wish he had someone to share what was on his mind. It didn't have to be a soul mate who could share his most intimate fears and frustrations; he would have been happy with anyone who would listen to him complain about his shoulders.

As time went on, Myron found the two or three friends he had were busy dealing with their own health problems and the uncertainty of their futures, so they were not emotionally available for support. Myron had increasing difficulty coping with the frustration caused by his aging body, so he really didn't feel like hearing more of the same from someone else anyway.

Only when Myron moved into the Pat Crowley House did he find the sympathetic ears that he needed. Curiously, he himself became more available emotionally.

Even as Trudy and Myron were being interviewed for this book, it was apparent from their willingness to counsel each other that their basic needs were being met. As Myron struggled to explain the malaise of retirement, Trudy tried to help.

"Once you're no longer useful to the world in general," she said, "it is kind of traumatic to lose all your responsibilities."

Grateful that she helped to clarify his thought, Myron continued.

"It is hard to get used to being retired," he said. "For so many years, you hop out of bed in the morning and get yourself ready and you go off to work. You get back at five or six. You get around here and there. And then suddenly there isn't any of that anymore. You just have to do whatever you can to fill up the time."

Myron stopped and sighed, still stumped by the impossible riddle of retirement idleness. He thought of what he used to do to cope before he found H.O.M.E.

"I would go to the zoo a lot," he said. I walked around in there and gazed at the animals. I guess I was looking for something to do."

Trudy thought retirees actually missed the scheduling they fought to keep up with all their lives. Myron agreed with her that retirement often meant the loss of a structure that had always been taken for granted.

"That kind of leaves us up in the air," he said. "Kind of floating around."

Both Trudy and Myron agreed that they needed to be close to people. Myron took walks around the block just to get out and be around other people, and Trudy rode the bus to malls. They weren't naive. They knew that lonely seniors were too often easy targets for unscrupulous salespersons or predatory criminals, but like many elderly people, their need for human contact far outweighed any risks they took. At H.O.M.E., they pointed out, they could leave their money lying around without fear of losing it.

Myron described another advantage of H.O.M.E. over the nursing home where he ended up after his stroke: noise level. The nursing home was more like a hospital, with people walking up and down the hall all night long, people screaming, the weird smells of institutional cleaners. All this sensory pollution wreaked havoc on his sensitive elderly nervous system. People with illnesses often say they are extremely reactive to certain stimuli like noises, smells, textures, or the quality of light. At H.O.M.E., Myron said he really appreciated having his own quiet bedroom.

Myron hated to think about what would have become of him had his caseworker and doctor not referred him to H.O.M.E., but he wondered anyway. He couldn't have signed himself out, or just left, since his status was more like "an inmate," as Trudy put it. Trudy explained the mechanism by which some seniors effectively became confined in nursing homes against their wishes. She knew how it went because it almost happened to her. When she got sick, her doctor explained that the nursing home was the only place for her to go because of her insurance. The nursing home came with its own doctor, so Trudy could no longer be seen by her regular physician. On a side note, one cannot help wondering how many in-house doctors would be naturally reluctant to discharge patients from the nursing home, or even to allow excursions in the outside world. They would not only be concerned with liability, but also with the financial interest of their employer. In the absence of an alternative, one could even excuse such a bias from a nursing home doctor. Trudy was lucky to be introduced to H.O.M.E., but how many of her contemporaries were left in the nursing home, unaware of any other resources.

Like other residents, Myron and Trudy wanted more elderly people to know about H.O.M.E. They realized that more homes for inter-generational shared living were needed to accommodate the aging American population, but they had some advice to avoid potential pitfalls in an expansion movement. Scale, they thought, was essential to the feeling of home they got.

"I don't think that you would have the camaraderie if there were too many people living here," Myron said.

The small size of the dwelling was probably the most significant factor in differentiating it from dehumanizing institutions. The large Nathalie Salmon House had less of a homey atmosphere, but daily life at the Pat Crowley House retained a familial quality because the residents could almost count their housemates on the fingers of their hands. The quality of life there was beyond comparison with any institutional setting. It was nice to have a schedule of activities, but most of the time, the simple fact of living together was entertaining enough. Trudy loved to ride the Silver Glide chairlift to the second floor at the Pat Crowley House to visit other residents. Right before Christmas, Trudy and several others went shopping together at a mall and had great fun. With over 1 million homes in the city of Chicago, it is reasonable to expect that there would be room for a residential movement like H.O.M.E. to expand.

During our interview, Myron diplomatically broached the sensitive but central topic of tolerance in communal life. The possibility of sharing a home with some people one disliked certainly existed, not unlike in conventional family situations. The H.O.M.E. experience differed from even the most mildly dysfunctional familial homes in that residents there actually tried to get along, because the harmony of the house was at the forefront of their consciousness.

"It is not a haven of love, but it is a showcase of tolerance," cofounder Michael Salmon liked to say.

Myron, who was probably less sociable than Trudy, noticed that people at H.O.M.E. felt empowered to express themselves honestly, without fear of retribution, so that differences were tolerated, and bonds grew naturally between some residents, and not between others.

"I am not close to any of my family anymore," Trudy said. "They are all gone."

Trudy lamented that some in her family used to question her about very private matters. She didn't feel that anyone had crossed the line with her since she'd moved into the Pat Crowley House. Myron ventured that since all the residents had similar interests, they knew better than to trample on each others' rights to privacy.

For Myron and Trudy, sharing a home with others like them (and unlike them) was an experience of maturation and deepening flexibility. Myron actually thought he had become more tolerant by living at the Pat Crowley House. He saw himself as more likely to be sympathetic with others and better able to understand their problems. Trudy also felt that the communal lifestyle had deepened her tolerance by showing her parts of her own character that were difficult for others to bear. They alternately saw others in their true light and glimpsed at mirror images of themselves.

"Myron didn't like the teasing at first," Trudy chided, "but now he sure teases back."

Because of the communal aspects of this form of housing, residents did not benefit alone from teachings. Caren, the house manager, also viewed tolerance as her most important lesson. She learned how much more important people are than material possessions. In the past, she might have procrastinated about calling someone, but H.O.M.E. showed her that human contact was important. As she opened up to others, she also paid closer attention to the quality of interactions; she tried not to let her occasional somber moods spoil things for others.

Thanks to the presence of Caren's children in the house, elderly residents were very much in tune with younger generations. They were sharply aware that Caren's children were the exception. Kids on the outside largely ignored them or even made fun of them at times. They wished that the attention they gave to the younger generation was mutual, but as they saw it, younger ones had a tendency to dismiss older people as inattentive and not especially sharp-witted.

"We're not just old geezers," Myron said.

Trudy blamed the neglectful attitude of young people on too much praise and ego. She and Myron noted that today's youth were more hostile than young people in the past, but Trudy was quick to point out that the students who helped at H.O.M.E. were different. They never used a patronizing tone with any of the residents and always valued their contributions.

Myron's advice to teenagers was to practice patience and empathy. "Young people act too quickly and are too quick to make judgments," he said. "And they could try and see other people's viewpoint once in a while."

As Myron quickly reviewed his life, he noted that he grew up during a much tougher time, when gratification was often delayed and material rewards were scarce. He had difficulty accepting the way young people so easily accumulate material possessions, especially cars.

Trudy was more empathetic, remarking that Myron grew up in the city, while country kids like herself needed cars to get around. Trudy even drove before she had a license, she said, out of necessity.

Myron jumped on the chance to tease her and intimated that he would report Trudy to the police, prompting Trudy to remind Myron that he had an unfortunate habit of stealing her dessert at the table. They both chuckled themselves to tears.

When they stopped bouncing up and down from laughing, Trudy wiped her eyes and, catching herself, declared seriously that this kind of bonding was what made H.O.M.E. such a positive, hopeful place. She added that residents also complemented each other when one had trouble remembering something.

Myron followed suit, with the thought that the way they lovingly teased each other suggested a second childhood, or at the very least a second chance.

"A place where no one takes away my world," added Trudy. "When I used to ride a bus from place to place, and just sit on the bench and watch people go by, I often sat right in front of the Nathalie Salmon House, looking toward the lake, and I didn't even know about it."

Bridging Generations

Caren, the program coordinator, did not have any family when she moved to Chicago with her husband. As she began raising her children in the city, she longed for the extended family system she enjoyed as a kid. She heard from a neighbor about an opening for a H.O.M.E. program coordinator, and moved upstairs with her husband and two children. Initially, she thought she would stay a couple of years, as a way of creating an extended family for herself and her children, but she ended up staying 11 years. The ties that formed in the community didn't stop when people left. Caren and her husband went to a former student helper's wedding and generally stayed in touch with the people who were part of their home. Residents who died were also remembered in conversations throughout the house. When Caren's mother-in-law died, residents had a white Japanese blossom tree planted in the garden of the Pat Crowley House in her memory.

Trudy found Caren to be an indefatigable help, a sort of super concierge who took residents to get prescriptions refilled before medicine ran out and was always available as a general resource. Trudy marveled at Caren's seemingly unending energy, but Caren didn't seem all that surprised, knowing that the place itself emanates a nourishing sense of warmth.

"It feels homey," Caren explained. "There are no slipcovers or plastic over furniture. We can toss a blanket on ourselves as we watch TV if we want to. It's the feeling of being comfortable and being at home." Caren's own family shared the top floor of the building with the four student helpers. Caren had to develop a wide array of abilities, from general medical knowledge to property management, social work, and counseling.

Although altruism could be seen as a suspicious motivation for people who chose to work in a human service field, Caren was clear about her reasons for choosing to live and work in this community. Unlike the usual professional settings where compensation was financial, staff in communities like H.O.M.E. are more likely to receive in-kind contributions of a qualitative nature. For example, Caren pointed out she intended to provide her own kids with a beneficial experience.

"Hopefully it has made them better people," she said.

Caren, who has a social sciences degree with a special education emphasis, noticed that her children were much more compassionate than most kids their age. Caren's children got a noticeable maturity from witnessing the effects of old age and from accepting the proximity of death as a fact of life. Most of their playmates were likely to be quite removed from the issue of death; they just knew that Grandma went to live in a home and never came back. Caren's children saw elderly residents still able to experience pleasure even as they grew near death. They saw that old age was a vulnerable time, and they secretly marveled at the fragility of life. They grieved with everyone in the house when someone died.

The four students also modeled compassion to Caren's children, who saw them taking care of the elderly residents every day, in between their college courses. The children made the family atmosphere in the house more real. It was not uncommon for an old man or woman to sit with a child to read a story or to play a board game. The presence of Caren's children in the house also encouraged children from the outside to interact with the residents, like the class of fourth graders who became pen pals and later had a party with them.

Neighbors could tell that the atmosphere inside the home was special, and they often became involved. The firefighters from the firehouse next door dropped in to borrow a cup of sugar. Not only were they available in case of emergency, but they also helped with shoveling snow around the house. Caren's husband returned the favor by mowing the grass on the parkway once in a while. The firefighters had some idle time spent waiting at the station, so in the summertime they played golf in the street and had water fights with the kids.

Other neighbors made it a habit to come in to chat. It was noted that people usually didn't drop in at a nursing home unless they were making a specific visit. The fact that the Pat Crowley House was part of a mainstream neighborhood invited people to become involved with the residents. The hairdresser who had a shop on the corner knew everyone, and she got some business from the house. It was as if people were afraid of nursing homes, whereas H.O.M.E. environments didn't scare them away. As Caren pointed out, people were afraid of death and did anything to avoid the question as a way of coping with their fear. Putting people in nursing homes made many feel more comfortable. Caren also accused her generation of being selfish in the way they prioritized their own fun, even at the expense of elders.

H.O.M.E. recreated the reality of the extended family. It was not a new idea—people who were not blood relations have always chosen to live together in communities and tribes—but it was implemented to counteract the failure of modern families and of Western society to care for their elders. Most of the people at H.O.M.E. were not close with their biological families. In cases where they were the lone survivors, distant relatives, friends, and social services failed to step in with truly helpful solutions.

As Caren said, her kids have had the luxury of having four big sisters and a dozen grandparents. Clearly, the four students also benefit by trading the prospect of a chaotic college dorm for this kinder, more dignified living arrangement. Students work two weekend days a month and help clean parts of the building twice a month. Each student is assigned one to three elderly residents and is responsible for cleaning their rooms and doing their laundry. During community night events, students are also expected to help. There are 12 individual rooms for the elderly H.O.M.E. residents. The rooms are grouped into three suites, with five rooms in the first-floor suite, four on the west side of the second floor, and three on the east side of the second floor (Caren's apartment and the student rooms are on the third floor). Each suite has a bathroom, a kitchen, and a living room with a TV. There is also a larger dining room on the first floor, where residents eat lunch and dinner together. The grouping in suites encourage a kind of synergetic dynamism: it reminds residents that they are part of a community that needs them. This community spirit is also practiced with the understanding that anyone who is not feeling well or prefers to be alone can find privacy in his or her room. This allows elderly residents to take a break from the four students or from Caren's two children. The children generally infuse a welcome energy into the place.

"The kids keep you hopping," said one resident. "I like them here."

According to residents, the intergenerational aspect of H.O.M.E. adds balance, which may seem elementary, but is in fact crucial in terms of its value. Because each age group is present in the household, it seems more complete, more natural. This physical reminder of the periodicity of life is the key to the wholeness of the H.O.M.E. environment.

"Life encompasses everything," H.O.M.E. founder Lilo Salmon said. "We should not separate age; that is not natural. What is natural is that people of all ages live together and learn from each other, care for each other."

Every age group must be represented to create wholeness in a community and to invite the natural process of healing to take place. Allen defined "the natural state of existence as whole," explaining that "disease is a condition of division and separation from the harmony of the whole. Beauty is wholeness. Health is wholeness. Goodness is wholeness" (1992, pp. 60, 61). It is also good for the rest of the natural world to be present, as H.O.M.E. residents found out with Patch, the resident dog. When Caren went on a vacation with her family, the residents told her to just leave Patch with them.

H.O.M.E. in the Media

It is difficult to convey an accurate picture of true communities to the world around them, yet it is an important part of encouraging the opening of new havens. H.O.M.E. was fortunate to attract the support of actor Bill Murray, who narrated a TV documentary about its community building efforts. *There's No Place Like H.O.M.E.* illustrated how the Pat Crowley House allowed seniors to break out of their isolation. Several residents were profiled in the documentary, which was used by H.O.M.E. in fundraising efforts. A documentary of this quality can go a long way in raising the consciousness of the public because, unlike the news media that bombard viewers with endless reports of inhumanity, this report shows pictures of human kindness and hope.

Viewers are easily won over by heartwarming characters like Billy, 95, who was on the road most of his life after his parents died when he was a teenager.

"I went to the school of hard knocks," Billy said, recalling the years he spent hopping on freight trains to travel around the country. At 81, Billy was still working, but he began having heart problems, and lived in and out of hospitals and nursing homes for the next few years.

Billy was a realist. He knew that H.O.M.E. greatly extended his life expectancy. "I might have died from the heat or the cold weather," he said. "The bugs would eat me up. If I wasn't here at the Crowley house, I would be dead a long time ago." H.O.M.E. was the first real home Billy ever had. From his bohemian life, he kept a tough but positive attitude.

"Don't be a crybaby! Get up on your own two legs and be somebody!" he dispensed to anyone who might be listening, before breaking into a song: "You are my sunshine, my only sunshine."

Reynolds was only 69, but he spent several years in a nursing home after a stroke left him disabled a few years into his retirement. Doctors were not hopeful that he would ever walk or talk again, but Reynolds was convinced that living at the Pat Crowley House transformed him.

"To strive, to seek, to fight and not to yield, and that's what I try to do," he declared from the wheelchair he used to get around.

Reynolds learned he couldn't do anything about the past, and he stopped feeling sorry for himself, as he put it. "I'm not interested in the past," he continued. "I'm interested in today and perhaps something of tomorrow."

Reynolds was fiercely independent because he understood the temptation of letting others do things for him was great. Even in the infamous Chicago winters, he managed to go where he wanted on his own. It was sometimes difficult for others not to help him, but they respected his choice and waited until he requested their assistance.

Reynolds was always vigilant that no one, not even a well-intentioned person, took away his autonomy.

"Nobody pushes me around," he deadpanned, wheeling himself back a few feet.

Other anecdotes abound, in which desperate elderly persons found H.O.M.E. and decided to stay. A woman was having serious difficulties with her family and needed another place to live. With no solution in sight, she contemplated pretending to be suicidal in order to be admitted to a mental hospital. That was when she came into the Pat Crowley House for a lunch and a trial visit. She ended up staying.

Sometimes, writers write about a community because they are themselves directly involved with H.O.M.E. *Chicago Tribune* writer Judy Marcus (2000) described her H.O.M.E. visit with her 83-year-old mother-in-law Faye. One of the residents took Judy's hand and said, "Don't worry about Mom. We'll take care of her." After Faye moved into the Nathalie Salmon Home, another resident helped her find her room one evening.

"Not to worry," the woman said to Faye. "I'll always be there to help you find your way."

It was apparent to Judy and Faye that the residents watched out for each other. As Judy wrote, "Muriel puts drops in Irene's vision-impaired eyes. Joan assists Faye, who has mild memory loss, with her medication. And Faye, who is able-bodied, helps anybody who could use a good set of arms and legs, whether to grab a juice glass or pick up a dropped magazine."

As one resident said in *There's No Place Like H.O.M.E.*, "You don't get that old feeling when you look out the window."

CHAPTER 4

A Retreat from Mental Illness: Learning the Art of Living

In the United States, about 400,000 people with chronic mental disorders reside in group homes or with their families. About 250,000 remain in mental hospitals, and many are in jails (Duffy & Wong, 2000). About 1.2 million individuals with mental illness reside in nursing homes, which is now the largest system of care for those who have a severe mental illnesses. Thousands of individuals with mental disorders are regularly released from state hospitals and detoxification programs with no place to go. Treatment for mental illness is often provided in a depersonalized manner that does not attend to individual needs. An unfortunate by-product of the distance and objectivity cultivated by many doctors, therapists, and nurses is that their patients feel like they are being processed rather than cared for. Fairweather (1979) noted that many patients with mental illness had little motivation and great institutional dependency. Behaviors that worked well in the hospital did not translate well to the community, and formerly hospitalized patients showed high rates of recidivism (Fairweather, 1979). When chronically mentally ill patients moved back into the community to live, they returned to the hospital at a rate of 70 percent to 75 percent, irrespective of the types of treatment they had received during hospitalization.

With statistics like these, it is not surprising that an organization that produced even mild improvements would attract members. We found people with severe and chronic mental illness who found a way to beat these statistics in southern Illinois. Not only were they willing to talk to us, but they also described their lives before and after their discovery of a grassroots organization called GROW.

The GROW organization started out in Sydney, Australia, in 1957 and expanded to New Zealand, Ireland, England, Mauritius, Singapore, Canada, and the United States. Originally, GROW was a group of psychiatric patients who banded together to rehabilitate themselves from the crippling effects of a mental health crisis. As they experienced success and improved their mental health, they decided to keep a record of the things they found most helpful. "You alone can do it," they proclaimed, "but you can't do it alone." Inspired by the success of Alcoholic Anonymous 12-step groups, they crafted a routine for their meetings and outlined an underlying philosophy.

Since then, GROW's driving force, friendship, has encouraged members to use as many of their personal resources as possible to reach their goal. In the 1998 reprint of its pamphlets, GROW describes its goal in everyday language: "maturity, or mental health," a quality that includes "a true mind, a loving heart, and a strong character." In order to achieve this maturity, and live life with "the vigour [*sic*] and peace of a person who is wholly attuned to reality," members are encouraged to develop "understanding, acceptance, confidence, control, and love." Rather than being born of a particular theoretical framework with its corresponding clinical lingo, the GROW philosophy was the collective product of lessons learned through direct life experience, and the copious GROW pamphlets were largely a matter of common sense. It was the sense that they could actually get reality-based answers to their mind-numbing questions that drew patients like Bruce to GROW. The expanding community was nondenominational and open to all, and members maintained anonymity. No membership fees or introductions were required. Voluntary participation in the weekly two-hour GROW meetings started involving more people with chronic mental suffering, who came for preventive medicine and a friendly community always willing to help.

Original members helped forge a helpful group structure. The first half hour of the group meeting was used to share some of the insight former and current members contributed to GROW's literature. The readings were then discussed in an open and general discussion, and served to reaffirm guiding principles. The rest of the meeting was devoted to individual problem solving.

GROW opened a residential center in Kankakee, Illinois, in 1985 to house its more seriously ill members. The center provided a home where residents could coach each other through GROW's "12-step Program of Personal Growth." By giving and receiving mutual support, the men and women who shared this home, and others like it, progressed through four levels of responsibility and corresponding privilege. Level one pertained to "orientation and personal responsibility" and consisted of specific ways to combat isolation. Level two introduced members to "leadership training" and interpersonal interactions. Level three invited residents to broaden their interactions outside of house boundaries by developing "community leadership and outreach." Level four was a transition to the outside community, where unsupervised living arrangements were made available by GROW. Each level was replete with practical goals and ways to achieve them, but the nature of the learning was experiential rather than didactic. As one of the many proverblike GROW mantras reminded staff and residents, "it can be caught, not taught." For example, level one residents were advised to develop "self-esteem through giving affirmation and encouragement, realizing each individual's importance as a connecting link in a community." At level three, residents were encouraged to obtain a driver's license or to enroll in academia or job training.

The GROW members we talked to told us their stories in the living room of the Kankakee house.

Bruce's Story

"It's a big world out there," Bruce started, nervously holding his meaty forearms in his hands. "You can do an awful lot of damage to yourself and to others."

Bruce explained that he didn't learn to communicate his true emotions in his family's abusive home. Understandably, the world where he was born, then where he was beaten and raped by relatives, did not invite him to open up. Early on, Bruce made a succession of survival adjustments. As a child, he learned to block out his pain by talking to an imaginary friend. When he joined the Navy at 17, right at the end of the Vietnam War, he was quickly introduced into drinking and getting high. The alcohol and drugs provided him with welcome relief from his psychic wounds. He couldn't just drink a little; he had to drink until he fell down, which led to a serious motorcycle accident. He was pronounced dead at the scene by paramedics, resuscitated, pronounced dead on arrival at the hospital, and brought back to life once more. After he recovered physically from the wreck, he decided to deepen his recovery by attending AA.

Bruce soon became a drug and alcohol counselor and got a bachelor's degree, but the more he counseled others for their addictions, the more his own unexamined mental illness was pushed to the fore of his consciousness. His powerful capacity for denial, reinforced by his role as a mental health professional, allowed Bruce to ignore his worsening symptoms. After three suicide attempts and florid hallucinations and delusions of being possessed by demons, he ended up in a state hospital, where he heard of GROW.

Bruce went to a few GROW groups after his discharge from the state psychiatric ward. From his sporadic attendance in GROW community groups, he understood that he needed to learn to be honest, to argue, and to disagree.

"I've got a lot of head knowledge," Bruce said, pointing his tattooed, ropy arm to his head and his chest. "But I've never been able to get it from my head to my heart."

Beaten into submission by mental illness, Bruce was willing to make the necessary sacrifices to find stability. Part of the GROW organization consisted of a communal home, where people like him could live together and support each other in their suffering. He decided he was ready to take direction from someone else and willing to give up his privacy (Bruce had a fiancée with whom he could have stayed instead). He made an appointment with a nearby GROW house and made his way there.

From the outside, the massive two-story Victorian frame house looks like many others in the small, rural town of Kankakee, an hour south of Chicago. A tall evergreen leans away from the freshly painted clapboard siding, like a soft sign pointing toward a few parking slots painted on the driveway of a detached garage, where a few stored items peer through a dusty window. As Bruce climbed the steps to the front door, he expected to be greeted by kids playing, but the porch was clear. There was not even a barking dog. Soon, a woman wiping her hands on her apron greeted him inquisitively through the screen door.

As he stepped inside, Bruce realized that this house's resemblance to others down the street was limited to its façade. This GROW, Inc., residential center housed a nontraditional family. Its residents were all adults unrelated to each other who shared the burden of mental illness and the need for a place to call home.

Bruce credited the balance of work, play, rest, eating, and studying inside the community for the healing he experienced. AA meetings alone were not enough. Once he moved into the GROW house, Bruce learned how to handle himself maturely and began to generalize his new way of being to the larger community. Before GROW, Bruce could not keep a job because his living arrangements did not provide enough psychological safety to keep his overwhelming childhood memories at bay. Whether he worked as a counselor or ran a pig farm, unexamined wounds resurfaced, and he would not show up at work, or he would fly into a rage if he got frustrated. Complete and honest disclosure was the norm for GROW residents, so Bruce never felt ridiculed or stigmatized for baring his soul. Residents talked about their illnesses in everyday terms, staying away from clinical labels.

"I learned to go by what I knew, not what I felt," Bruce explained, quoting GROW's own phrasing. "So instead of raging on a piece of equipment I couldn't fix, I remembered I could do it after I calmed down."

The GROW house was more like an artist's retreat than a treatment program. People went there to retreat from the outside world and to work on their masterpieces: their own lives. The communal aspect of their daily interactions with other residents had more in common with writing workshops, where artists give each other feedback on ways to improve their respective work, than with the counseling dispensed by a therapeutic authority.

Bruce was surprised by how well people got along in the house, considering they were always in each other's company. People were at once able to follow a familiar routine and to cope with unexpected changes. Bruce found the daily household routine to be a reliable support, a guardrail that kept him on the road to rehabilitation, away from the pathological extremes of paralysis and extreme change. That link people felt with each other inside the house as they completed everyday tasks together was very spiritual to Bruce. The subtle levels of mutual support achieved inside the GROW house started with physical proximity and shared routines.

The Balance between Individual Needs and the Good of the Community

Most residents took three to four years to regain the strength they needed to function in the world at large. They gradually transitioned from their community to the world around it, but Maureen clearly considered herself a permanent resident in the Kankakee house. Staff members were quick to point out that, considering the immense progress they had witnessed Maureen make, hers was still a success story. When she arrived at the house after a lifetime of institutionalization, she only paced around, gritting her teeth and clutching her handbag. Since then, although she still gripped her bag wherever she went, she relaxed enough to function with the other 10 residents.

In 2002, the monthly rent was set at two-thirds of the resident's income—usually a monthly disability payment—or $290, whichever was less. This included room and board (a typical lunch consisted of chipped beef on two slices of white bread and a cup of Kool-Aid), and access to a laundry room and any of the common areas of the house. These privileges came with the responsibility for shared house chores. Residents were also required to have $100 for monthly outings like bowling or movies. No one was ever turned away for lack of income, but most of these residents paid back GROW once they felt better. New residents were all given checking accounts and taught how to manage their meager incomes.

Sylvia's Story

As a testament to the therapeutic efficacy of their environment, other residents have made impressive recoveries as well. When Sylvia arrived at the Kankakee house, she had been hospitalized on psychiatric wards about 30 times, for as long as three months at a time. She had lived in a group home and a nursing home, and she even lived with her sister for a while. None of these living arrangements and treatment solutions kept her from wanting to kill herself or from cutting deep gashes in her arms with whatever sharp instrument she could lay her hands on. Sylvia had a foggy memory of her time in the nursing home because she was so ill that she slept 18 to 20 hours a day. She stayed up from 2 A.M. to 6 A.M. watching *MASH* reruns. With the nursing home's dollar-a-day allowance, she could not go on any of the outings. Group schedules were unreliable, and nursing home staff members stopped coming to get her for groups anyway. It's not like Sylvia was missing much anyway: the finance group consisted of making patients count change.

"They'd say 'count out 23 cents,'" Sylvia remembered. "And I would count out 23 cents."

In another patronizing scenario, patients were told, "This costs $1.25. How much are you gonna give me?"

"I have, on a couple occasions, hit my head on concrete walls," Sylvia recalled.

Before Sylvia's coping skills became overwhelmed by psychiatric symptoms in her late twenties, she worked as a hospital nurse, until she began experiencing terrifying flashbacks of the sexual abuse she had endured at the hands of her older brother and a neighbor.

By her own account, Sylvia's life was changed when she moved into the GROW house. At first, Sylvia listened. She enjoyed not being forced to speak. It felt good just to be there, in the company of other residents. The daily morning exercise (7:10 A.M.–8:00 A.M.) and the rest of the daily schedule (7 A.M. to 9 P.M.) took some getting used to—Sylvia was so obese that she could hardly move around—and the smallest criticism made Sylvia break down in tears. Gradually, she learned to reserve such intense emotional displays for situations that warranted them. The quality of the interactions she experienced in the GROW house won her over.

"There's so much care," Sylvia tried to explain. "It's almost indescribable, really!"

Compared to the nursing home, where she had no friends and where burned-out counselors learned to avoid her, the GROW house has ushered Sylvia into an unparalleled quality of relationship. By her own account, none of Sylvia's prior treatments—even radical and aggressive options like electroconvulsive therapy (ECT)—had been as successful in lifting her depression as this form of community living. For the GROW finance group, Sylvia was given her own checkbook and coached on how to manage her income. She beamed as she explained how much better GROW worked for her.

"I'm known as the budget queen," she said, relating how satisfying it was for her to be able to in turn teach her roommates simple things like budgeting.

Tim's Story

Another resident, Tim, was quick to acknowledge how much he learned from Sylvia, among others. "When I first came here, I couldn't boil an egg," Tim said excitedly. "I didn't know the right way to peel a potato, or follow a recipe, or even how to write a check. I couldn't have made it on my own. I learned how to do all that confidently. I even started running the kitchen."

Tim explained how he still learned from his mistakes, like the meat that went bad when he forgot to plug the freezer back in. The feeling of community that filled the GROW house had given his ego enough flexibility to weather previously overwhelming frustrations. Although

Tim's appearance was youthful, he had the fluency of someone with several years of distance from his story.

"I was the perfect child," Tim started without hesitation. "All my mom had to do was look at me wrong and I would cry."

Tim started to rebel at age 12, after changing school districts, and "got in with the wrong crowd," seeking attention by getting into trouble. Tim soon landed in jail for stealing cars and for an uninterrupted stream of petty theft and vandalism. Neither Tim's juvenile probation officer nor his family could stop his self-destructive need for attention. He stole apples from people's yards, threw rocks at cars, and even got caught breaking into a church to steal wine.

One of the relatively healthy ways Tim sought attention was by driving a hot rod to high school. It was a muscle car he had entirely built himself and maintained meticulously. Tim's brother and sister were largely indifferent to his shenanigans, but that changed when Tim turned 15. As soon as Tim was diagnosed with Hodgkin's lymphoma, a form of cancer he blamed on the anabolic steroids he took to keep up with his bodybuilding classmates, he got all the attention in the family. Once again, something negative supplied Tim with all the care and consideration he craved. Tim's siblings remained estranged.

"I can't talk to either one of them," Tim said. "Because I'm mentally ill; they don't understand."

With the benefit of hindsight, Tim supposes the source of his mental breakdown was a combination of stress and chemotherapy. Tim was placed in a nursing home. He got up at five every morning, and unlike the other nursing home residents, he kept a job at a drive-through fast-food joint. His manic energy allowed him to do all the tasks so fast that he actually exceeded the inhumane corporate productivity standards, and this earned him an employee of the month award soon after he started working there. He got to work an hour early and did crossword puzzles until it was time to punch in. When he wasn't at work, Tim lay on the vinyl couch in a nearby day program and smoked cigarettes. He went to groups reluctantly, lamenting over the dismal quality of these therapeutic encounters.

"They are not groups to get better," Tim said. "They're just warehouses. They just bring you there, and they get paid by the state if a certain amount of people go to their group."

Tim remembers not being able to put a word in edgewise during overcrowded groups. Then there were empty promises made to him by program staff, presumably to motivate him: a subsidized home, big money, a job in the community.

"I suppose they had the best intentions," Tim concedes. "But they never followed through!"

When he first contacted the GROW house for living arrangements, he was allowed to spend a few days on a trial basis.

"I was so hyper," Tim remembered. "They were scraping me off the walls."

Gradually, Tim was accepted into the house. He immediately contrasted the GROW house with his previous experiences: GROW was his home, his family, which was helping him get better. The rent was affordable; other GROW residents and team leaders gently and supportively pushed Tim to go to college, coaching him about money management.

"GROW is the best thing I've ever done for myself," Tim said. Tim views his newly found ability to control his temper as his biggest conquest. Without it, Tim is certain he would have been killed already. He had spent much of his time in psychiatric wards in full restraints. Back on the outside, very few people could tolerate his boisterous outbursts, and he frequently met with violent reactions. Even when he arrived at the GROW house, he rubbed everyone the wrong way. Only once Tim learned to deal with stress and anger could people tolerate him.

"They started to like me," Tim said. "And I started to like myself." As he put it, they loved him back to mental health.

Lucy's Story

Another resident, Lucy, moved into the GROW residence as an alternative to hospitalization for major depression and suicide attempts. At the time, Lucy's psychiatrist gave her a grim prognosis: she would be able to function minimally, and she would have to take psychotropic medication for the rest of her life. The GROW residence allowed her to achieve much more than that, leaving that prognosis far behind. For someone like Lucy who had become fearful and avoidant of people following sexual abuse as a child, it was helpful to experience care and empathy without having to leave home. She could receive the nurturing she needed without triggering paralyzing panic attacks. The house's daily schedule provided her with reliable expectations at first, but she became dependent on it and the slightest variation caused her great distress. As she learned to accept schedule changes, she became more flexible. As Lucy gradually regained strength and confidence, other residents invited her to help with some of the administrative work for the house. Unsure that she could be of any help, she took on some of the office work, and ended up gradually assuming most of the house's operational clerical tasks. She was certain that without the GROW community that welcomed her, she would have either succeeded in a suicide attempt or been placed in a nursing home by relatives unable to cope with her mental illness. Not only did community living give Lucy her psychological health back; it also rehabilitated her socially and financially, after traditional biomedical treatment left her high and dry. GROW treated Lucy as a whole being. Consequently, the healing extended beyond Lucy's personal boundaries, spreading back to Lucy's family members, who had become estranged.

GROW's Successes and Challenges

One after the other, the GROW residents we talked to reported the same satisfaction. The GROW house was not only the most efficient treatment they had ever received, but it was also the best living situation. The best part was that these superior residential and treatment benefits were rolled into one and integrated into their day-to-day lives.

Unlike the world at large, GROW house community members were able to see the humanity of new residents, even as it hid under the repellant layers of mental disease. This unconditional acceptance invited residents to open their hearts to others, and to use their energy to heal from their wounds rather than hide them.

Although the program was not a religious one, it was usually a spiritual experience for its residents. For Lucy, whose hardships had caused her to stop believing in God, communal living was the beginning of spiritual rehabilitation.

"I had a belief in the people around me," Lucy said. "The people were my spiritual support system."

Lucy's faith had been replaced by bitterness and cynicism, but from the healing and joy she experienced with others, Lucy eventually mended her relationship with God.

Like Oxford House, GROW developed rather organically, as people found ways to meet their own needs, but the two communities differed in the way they were funded. The financial independence of Oxford House from any governmental funding, except for the startup loan program, afforded it a remarkable stability regardless of market fluctuations. GROW's success attracted governmental funding, which

GROW chose to add to its list of private donors. Unfortunately, 2002 state funding cuts gave the Kankakee GROW house reason to worry. Residential program staff members Pam Fisher and Dianne Maxwell mused on the irony of funding cuts: Money seemed to be consistently cut from programs that worked well and cost little, while expensive and inefficient hospital-based treatment options retained their funding. The size of an organization's budget was unfortunately seen as a reflection of its success, independent of the outcome of its mission. Consequently, very successful groups with small budgets were overlooked, while heavily budgeted organizations gained respect in spite of sizable failures. During our interview, Bruce noted that, with the daily cost of $1,300 to $1,400 to hospitalize one person in a state inpatient mental ward, 16 people could be housed in two GROW houses for one month. As Bruce put it, the person in the state hospital "would get medicated and herded around," while the 16 people in the GROW house would not only heal old wounds but would also receive preventive treatment to stay out of the hospital. Fortunately, a grassroots coalition of people was successful in ensuring that funds would remain available for the GROW house to continue providing a haven.

Not surprisingly, self-run organizations for people with mental illness have not been the most assertive in making themselves known; residents and staff have been too busy ensuring that rehabilitation actually took place to lobby governments. The dominant concerns within the GROW community were actually far removed from the realm of the political (the preservation of self-interest through manipulation). Even if they had time, it would be unrealistic to expect the same people to operate simultaneously in the contrary worlds of community building and interest group lobbying. Moreover, people with mental illness are rarely granted the status of authority, even when they have found successful solutions. More often, they are expected to get better, while being denied the right to redefine who they are.

Not only did the inherent nature of GROW and other similar communities exclude them from funding decisions, but it also exposed them to the adversarial scrutiny of governmental regulatory agencies. Governmental funding came with strings attached, as the Kankakee GROW staff soon found out. They were more than willing to comply with the Kafkaesque mountain of guidelines and regulations—mostly having to do with documenting every aspect of treatment—but felt like their community was losing part of its soul in the process. For one thing, what they did was not treatment, but rather rehabilitation through the common tasks of everyday life—"a school for living," as Pam Fisher explained. Charting such fluid and natural phenomena as the act of being together and developing friendships proved dauntingly absurd. Making friends at home was definitely therapeutic for the residents, but it was not an activity to be charted; it was a necessary part of life. The act of documenting that organic process introduced a lethal deconstruction that might have killed the magic of the experience, but the state saw the house in a professional context, so GROW staff felt they had no choice. Through trial and error, they eventually learned to fulfill state requirements without sacrificing the daily work that was being done inside the house. They were pretty proud of mastering the art of documenting according to state guidelines. That's when the state cut their funding.

Ironically, the professional status that state regulators forced on communities like GROW was precisely what causes more traditional treatment settings to fall short of what mental patients really needed. All the mental patients we talked to agreed that mental health professionals simply do not have the time to provide them with the depth of relationship they need to heal. More importantly, most professionals would feel it is not their place to give patients the love they need and receive in the GROW community.

GROW residents got necessary medications prescribed by a psychiatrist, but all the psychological work was done in-house, by the residents themselves. Lucy pointed out that in some cases, outside professional therapists who didn't understand the GROW community created obstacles to the successful integration of new residents. As most therapists will do, they validated the complaints of new residents and reinforced their resistance to the community values and to the required sacrifices.

"What goes on in here is gut-level learning," Bruce explained. Most outside therapists, he continued, were unable to provide psychotherapy that was compatible with the intensity and the everyday nature of the GROW experience.

"There is that rare professional out there," Bruce acknowledged. As someone who knew the mental health care system both as provider and recipient, he was careful not to overgeneralize. "But the system itself is not user-friendly. It is very frightening, stigmatizing, and discriminatory."

Bruce attributed the shortcomings of the mental health system to the natural weakness of the humans who make up that system, and their tendency to distance themselves from patients as a protective measure. The danger in such an emotionally intense field, Bruce explained, is that the unordinary things professionals are confronted with for eight hours everyday became the norm. The inability to make this distinction, according to Bruce, marks the beginning of burn-out and the strengthening of alienating strategies for professional survival. According to Bruce, another cause of the system's desensitization to the vital needs of patients is that many policymakers and administrators are out of touch with patients.

"They don't understand the fear of walking into the unemployment office, or Public Aid, or Social Security, and asking for help," Bruce explained.

Patients noticed this happening across the supposed continuum of care. Bruce noted that hospitals were merely "warehouses that did not supply patients in crisis with ways to successfully transition from the hospital to the world at large."

Bruce noted his own traumatic discharge from five months of hospitalization in a state facility. With no money (he had not worked in over six months), he had to go to a homeless shelter. The first night there, all his belongings were stolen, triggering full-blown paranoia.

Ironically, policymakers looking for corners to cut might see the success of therapeutic communities as an opportunity for more funding cuts. If patients can get better on their own, they might think, they don't need our help.

Maybe part of the problem is that we grant the honorific title of *community* to the world at large, when it frequently offers no support to the people who are most in need and most vulnerable. Patients are shuffled from one traumatizing institution to another, until they are ejected into "the community." When they are condemned yet another time for "failing to function" in this world, they are taking the fall for society's failure to meet their vital needs for safety and support. The term *community* should be used sparingly, with the exception of a few rare places like the ones identified in this book and the many others that exist in anonymity.

Just as Bruce, Lucy, and Sylvia did not ask to be raped when they were children, they did nothing to deserve their lifelong struggle with mental illness. Their needs were pressing because their pain was so great, not because they somehow did not deserve help. Why should we, as productive members of society, tolerate the neglect of people in need, particularly when they can so clearly articulate what can help them?

Fortunately for Bruce, Lucy, and Sylvia, a community of healing was available. Their stories demonstrate what creates hope for people in hostile and compromising environments. The GROW house is a powerful model of what could be offered to millions of people with mental illness.

CHAPTER 5

THE INVISIBLE PATIENT

If you have a chronic health condition, you are one of over 90 million Americans. The prevalence of chronic illness has been rising steadily among men and women (Centers for Disease Control, 2000). If there is anything worse than suffering from a health condition, it is not being able to give it a name. For 30 percent to 80 percent of medical patients, there is no definitive diagnosis. As an example, 80 percent of patients with lower back pain have no identified cause of their pain (Muller, 2001). This is frustrating for patients, but it also complicates the job of treatment providers. Chronic ailments like chronic fatigue syndrome (CFS), fibromyalgia (FM), multiple sclerosis (MS), multiple chemical sensitivities (MCS), headaches, sleep disorders, and irritable bowel syndrome often pose unsolvable riddles to the health care system when they are severe.

One of the most debilitating of these chronic illnesses is chronic fatigue syndrome (Jason, Richman et al., 1997). It is not an illness that gets a lot of press, but you may have heard about it because Laura Hillenbrand, the author of the popular book *Seabiscuit*, is afflicted by CFS. Although from the outside, people with CFS often appear relatively well, they describe feeling as if poison is running through their veins. Health care professionals with CFS have likened it to life during the last six months of AIDS. The experience of suffering from CFS often proves overwhelming for everyone involved, but for the person who is ill, it can result in social isolation (Jason, Kolak et al., 2001).

Employers don't make allowances for a health problem that is seen as suspect, and sometimes use absenteeism and lack of productivity as reasons to terminate the ill employee. This is made worse by the fact that many patients with CFS often appear healthy. Health plans often deny coverage for the same reasons, and the patients feel stigmatized and invalidated by medical professionals. Marriages and friendships are tested by repeated calls for help and by an inability to pull one's weight, figuratively and even literally. Patients with CFS who are single or without a wide circle of friends are especially vulnerable. Spiraling medical bills and fatigue alone can quickly push someone into homelessness. Even if people with CFS have no psychological problems to begin with, it is easy to see how they could become depressed from what they go through (Friedberg & Jason, 1998).

Scientists in the early 1990s considered CFS to be a relatively rare disorder, affecting primarily white, middle-class women, but the way samples were gathered was later found to be misrepresentative. Once the perspective of patients with CFS was considered more carefully (see Appendix G for more information about this process), researchers working from balanced samples with better methodologies found that CFS is one of the most common chronic health conditions, affecting as many as 800,000 people in the United States (Jason, Richman et al., 1999). Rates are even higher for minorities. From 85 percent to 90 percent of individuals with this illness have never even been diagnosed with CFS.

Whatever the cause of CFS, it appears that the importance of environment in treatment is huge. People with CFS will tell you that the ideal treatment setting resembles a retreat more than a clinic. As we noted in the previous chapters, traditional treatment settings can fail in their purpose. For CFS, much of our health care system has missed the mark. The treatment outcomes for patients with CFS is discouraging: only 3 percent report complete recovery, and 17 percent report some improvement. These poor results are attributed to a lack of effective support in the patient's community. For many years, the consequences of inadequate housing have continued to plague those with controversial disabilities, such as CFS. These individuals are not only fatigued but also have multiple medical complaints that often lower their quality of life to the extreme. Many medical personnel and social service agencies question the legitimacy of these conditions, and affordable housing is rarely provided.

Jim's Story

The voices approaching along the narrow dirt path that followed the river were accompanied by the hum of cicadas. Jim walked a few steps ahead of his friend Beatrice, in the middle of an animated discussion. Once again, Beatrice was challenging his atheist views, and he shot answers back at her over his shoulder. Jim looked up through the lush canopy of trees and taunted God in the heavens.

"I doubt that you exist," he exclaimed dramatically. "But if you do, you can never harm me!"

"You should never say such things because the gods might retaliate," Beatrice said sternly.

Jim laughed off her superstitious concerns. Three months later, he couldn't move, confined to bed by a debilitating and puzzling fatigue. It was more than a lack of energy. Jim was not getting over a cold, as some of his friends believed. He simply did not have the energy to move more than a few times a day, and the slightest amount of work completely depleted him.

The next few years of Jim's life were completely transformed. Before he started feeling sick, his world had been predictable and his life devoted to work. Jim was well known locally as an administrator. He was reputed for being active, hardworking, and successful. The sudden fatigue forced him to reexamine the values that provided meaning to his life.

In many ways, Jim fit the typical profile of a high achiever. He supervised around 20 people at work, and loved each one of his many activities. Though he swam a quarter of a mile three times each week and ate properly, he had noticed that over the past few years he got colds and sore throats more often and had more difficulty getting over them. Ignoring these warning signs from his immune system, he increased his responsibilities rather than slowing down. Throughout his life he had grown used to spending time very productively.

On some level, Jim knew there was a problem, because in addition to the colds, he was beginning to feel drained at the end of the day. The first week of August, Jim noticed he had a persistent sore throat. By October, the sore throat worsened. The weather got colder. Jim's physician prescribed antibiotics, but they didn't help. Jim started having trouble keeping up with his work schedule, which required three out-of-town trips that month. Finally, at the beginning of November, he realized that this illness was different from anything else he had ever had. After a particularly stressful trip out of town, he decided to stay home and get well. After two weeks at home, he felt somewhat better, and his physician's diagnosis of mononucleosis seemed to bring closure to the episode.

Still, when Jim talked on the telephone for more than two hours, he was much weaker the next day. Following his doctor's suggestion, he returned to his office for the first time in three weeks, where he worked for about an hour and a half. Strangely, he came home exhausted. A few days later, his job required him to spend more time on the telephone than his body could stand. He stayed in bed the whole next day.

By late November, he could not write for more than five or ten minutes without collapsing with fatigue. Other troubling symptoms began to emerge. Insomnia kept him awake for long nights; he tossed and turned, soaking the sheets with sweat. Some nights in December, he stayed awake the entire night. Jim soon developed extreme sensitivity to light, to the extent that he could not bear to watch television. Even the light streaming in from the window became unbearable. He began feeling nauseated, and he began losing weight (20 pounds in the next two months) once his digestion soured. His tongue turned white, and his lymph nodes swelled. More and more, his memory and concentration failed him.

Beside the general physical discomfort he was in, he felt completely cut off from his work and friends. He hired a former employee to bring him food, but all his energy was consumed in getting up and preparing meals for himself. Having developed a sore back from lying in his bed for too long, he now spent his days lying on the floor and listening to the radio. He could not watch television or read. He could not take out the garbage. He could only speak to two or three people for five to ten minutes on the telephone, or risk complete exhaustion.

Jim had never felt so alone in his life. As weeks passed with no improvements, he realized he had an illness more serious than anything he had ever imagined, maybe even chronic fatigue syndrome (CFS). No amount of rest seemed to bring relief. Increasingly desperate for some possible solutions, Jim tried meditation, humor, and spiritual tapes, but they provided only temporary distraction. Tense and depressed, Jim had no idea how to improve his condition. His physician continued to assure him that he would get better with rest. In fact, Jim was not getting better and continued to see more signs of his body breaking down.

Weeks passed. Outside, leaves, then snow, fell to the ground. Lying on his floor, Jim stared at the ceiling, listening to the crunching footsteps of people walking to work in the morning. During the day, he coped with the absurdity of this new nightmare by wishing that he would wake from it. He had entered a new reality, one with no firm foundation. At night, feverish thoughts and feelings crowded his mind. When he finally toppled into sleep, vivid nightmares awoke him. In one of them, a monstrous devil appeared in the window and entered the apartment. As Jim woke up, the demon receded into the walls. Jim wondered if he could endure. An evil force had overcome his most creative quality, his very life force.

In spite of his growing loneliness, Jim resisted going to a self-help group. He feared that talking to other people who suffered from CFS might only demoralize him and make him more tired. He needed to talk to people who had recovered from this illness. In late December, he finally decided to contact people who belonged to self-help groups. These three people had been sick for many years, and they informed him that CFS left no choice but to accept low energy and loss of career. They said that many people with CFS had left work and were obtaining Social Security disability payments. That was exactly what Jim feared. The confirmation was shocking, but he still refused to believe that his fate was decided.

Jim felt alone, isolated, and scared. Several times a week, a few friends would visit him, but he became exhausted even by their brief conversations. His situation was so extreme that he was unsure of how much he could share with his friends. Even well-meaning friends were perplexed by his mysterious illness, and sometimes hesitant to help.

After Jim tried to inform a friend of how painful and difficult his life had become, the friend asked Jim if he was going crazy. Jim was not crazy, in spite of a crazy-making situation. He was in severe physical pain, but his mental faculties were relatively intact.

Another friend suggested that Jim should consider a less stressful job, like flipping hamburgers. Someone else thought that Jim looked too good to be ill and accused him of blowing everything out of proportion.

"Everybody gets colds and sore throats," he said. "What's the big deal? Why can't you do more?"

Colleagues pronounced him agoraphobic because he never left his apartment. People commented on his pale looks and advised him to get some therapy, to see a psychiatrist, to go on disability.

"Why do you sleep so much?" a friend asked suspiciously. "It's all in your mind," another assured him.

Some people, afraid that CFS was contagious, stopped visiting Jim. Colleagues blamed Jim for his condition, even lamenting that someone with his interest in prevention had obviously not practiced what he preached.

Gradually, the support of Jim's friends dwindled, as they reached their capacity for compassion.

"Things could be worse," they said in their attempts to minimize.

Jim tried in vain to educate his friends and colleagues about CFS, now that he was starting to be familiar with it.

"I'm bored with your conversations about chronic fatigue," a colleague said. "I resent you giving me an article on CFS, and I have no interest in the topic."

By then, Jim was feeling so vulnerable that the smallest annoyance left him deeply disturbed. In *Beaches*, a movie he watched at a friend's house, the main character dies of a virus that had previously caused her fatigue. Jim felt devastated after the movie, a reaction his friends could not understand.

Seeing many friends driven away by his state of mind, Jim wrote letters—one way of communicating that he could still manage. "I am a pygmy in a world of giants, trying to evade their smothering steps," he wrote. "Can any other disease make us look so well, but feel so sick inside? Has the devil incarnate cursed me 'til the end of my days?" Jim found the absurdity of the whole situation maddening. He had no idea what caused the oppressive fatigue that exhausted him, and it could be defined only subjectively. His experience felt real, but seemed imagined from the outside. Unable to pinpoint a cause for the illness, Jim blamed himself and withdrew even from the few who were still willing to share his pain. His best friend confronted Jim, asking why he shut her out of his life, and Jim answered her in another letter. "I am running from devils I have created. My isolation is so intense that it has no room for even you, my dearest friend. Each day for me is more death than life, for now I live in an underworld inhabited by bad dreams and despair." Jim ended the letter like a prisoner writing to his lover. "Please wait. I love you."

Ironically, Jim found himself in a position described exquisitely well in the writings of one of his favorite authors, Kat Duff (1993). Illness was indeed "a world of its own," with "its own geography beneath depths of darkness, its own gravity at the farthest bottom of life."

By late December, the frigid weather trapped Jim in his condominium for several months. He lay on his couch, trying to forget the painful welts that had sprouted on his arms from food allergies, when he began to experience breathing difficulties. "I have to get out of here," he thought, "or I'll just die on this couch." A friend told him of a week-long clinic on the East Coast that had success in treating people with chronic fatigue syndrome. Anything sounded better than wasting away in his own apartment. A few weeks later, Jim made up his mind to travel to the clinic.

Alternative Medicine

Jim was terrified at the idea of walking into the cold outside, and he wondered if he had the energy to make the trip. He feared he might get even sicker by pushing himself through the trip, but staying put had not helped either. The friend who drove him to the airport gave him a magazine article that warned patients with CFS of unscrupulous physicians who required patients to travel to their clinics. "Why is he giving me this now?" Jim thought. "I need to believe in something."

At the clinic, Jim seemed to have less energy than any of the 10 other CFS-afflicted people. They were all engaged in lively conversation. Every time Jim started to talk with someone, he had to walk away, feeling exhausted. Around seven, everyone got up and started walking to a nearby cottage for dinner—the clinic made arrangements with a local hostelry for room and board. Jim was gripped by the uncontrollable fear that he might not be able to keep up. It was one thing to get sick to his stomach after eating at home, but the prospect of vomiting helplessly on the table in front of 10 people was paralyzing. Jim also feared not having the energy to talk to the other people during supper, especially when it took so much just to chew and swallow the food. Would the others think he was antisocial? He began to cry. Never had he felt so alone, so dysfunctional, so crippled. After a few minutes, he made his way to the dining area, sat in a chair, and told the people at his table he would not be able to talk. With relief, he watched as everyone acknowledged and accepted him. Jim ate and then went to his room to try to sleep.

Jim quickly realized this experience would turn out to be positive. The others had been sick much longer than he had. He asked questions and learned about CFS. Being in a supportive and loving community of people who were like him was invigorating. Jim felt more alive than he had in months. The highlights of his week were two wonderful sessions with a psychotherapist. She was a warm, friendly, and inspiring person who had recovered from CFS. She so completely understood Jim's fears and anxieties that he continued his sessions by telephone after he left.

One evening, the patients went out to a restaurant for dinner; everyone except Jim, who did not have the energy to join them. He sat by the stone fireplace in the rustic cottage and proceeded to light a fire. After stacking up a couple logs over a handful of kindling, which took all the energy he had, he struck a match and watched as a small fire rose and sputtered out. God, I really want this fire, he thought collapsing in the rattan chair, but I cannot make it myself. He craned his neck in search of a helpful hand, but everyone in the guest house was out. Jim thought, "I'll just sit here and it will all be OK." Suddenly, like magic, a flame appeared and grew under the logs. Jim was struck by the symbolic significance of the moment. When he stopped trying to light the fire and accepted the situation, the wood burst into flames. The world was full of healing messages, he thought, as the fire warmed his skin. It was up to him to feel them.

As far as Jim could remember, he had allowed himself very little rest in any work situation. Jim could now see this process was too stressful; he finally understood that the gratification he derived from producing massive amounts of work was not worth sacrificing his own health. In order to stay on a self-sustaining path, Jim needed to let his heart be the guide.

Jim's mind was spinning with questions. Had his body revolted against a life crowded with material gain and increasingly devoid of the spiritual? Was this chronic disease an opportunity to leave behind an increasingly materialistic life? Were these questions just a way to cope with his loss of control? Perhaps the truth lay somewhere in between. As a high-achieving professional, Jim knew all too well how most people lived increasingly faster lives, driven out of control by evolving technology and an unexamined work ethic. This imbalance alone could lead to disease. There had to be a lesson in Jim's predicament. CFS could become a sort of anchor; in a way, it stabilized his life long enough for balance to reestablish itself.

The images elicited by these questions were helpful. CFS had rendered Jim painfully aware of the stress he used to take for granted. Stress was now a constant assault, like a water cannon shooting water at him. He could try to dam the gushing water, but that seemed like a futile and exhausting effort. He could try to dodge the stream of water, also a waste of energy. Or Jim could stop worrying about the impact of stress on his life, letting the water roll off his back. Stress was only stressful if you tried to control it.

During brief daily walks, Jim looked up at the sky and pretended to be an eagle. Once, as he walked down a rocky path, he spread his arms wide and thought about what it would be like to really soar above the world.

"I am a little bit higher," he said to himself. "I can look down and not be affected by daily issues. I can be above the stress. I do not have to be subjected to the ebbs and flows of life."

Jim also credited the healing quality of that week on the East Coast to the support he received from other patients. On the other hand, Jim was not completely sold on the clinic. He found out from one of the people in the clinic about another CFS self-help group that met nearby. None of the self-help group members were interested in the clinic where Jim was a patient. If the treatment program had a 90 percent success rate, as its pamphlet advertised, why wouldn't the other CFS patients who lived so close patronize it? Jim suspected that the clinic exaggerated its claims, but he also needed to believe that it would work for him.

Returning Home

After a week, Jim left the clinic and said good-bye to the group of CFS patients. It was difficult to leave them, not just because they were connected with the bonds of shared pain, but also because that single week had made him feel more alive and more hopeful than he had been in months. He wondered if he could continue recovering at his home. His wishes for just one more chance at life turned to a prayer. If he could regain his energy, he would value every morsel of the sweet life he had almost lost. His workaholic days would be gone.

He decided to trim his own shaggy hair. For about 10 minutes, he held his arms over his head, pulling his curly locks away from his head and snipping them off, awkwardly watching the mirror image of his handiwork. He soon felt so drained that he had to rest. There was proof that it was not all in his head, he thought. Even a mind filled with positive thoughts could not relieve his sick body.

The next three months were difficult. The mild surge of energy he had brought back from his week at the CFS clinic evaporated. The nausea came back; the stomach and intestinal problems recurred; and he again experienced sleepless nights, drenched in sweat. The slightest activity, like washing a couple of dishes, overwhelmed Jim with fatigue. By the end of February, he was back to the worst days of his sickness. Jim's doctor had more bad news: laboratory test results for the Epstein-Barr virus showed that he had been exposed to the virus. Another test result suggested that Jim was becoming allergic to many types of food. With advice from a nutritionist, he eliminated all the foods that could cause allergy. For the next four months, Jim ate no milk, eggs, wheat, corn, sugar, chocolate and colas, citrus, coffee, teas, alcohol, yeast, colorings, flavorings, or additives. Only then, did he gradually start introducing new foods back into his diet, painstakingly noting which foods caused his skin to erupt.

Jim continued to talk on the phone with the CFS clinic therapist. Jim found regular inspiration in her words and thought of her as a spiritual mentor. She encouraged Jim to meditate regularly and distance himself from his daily stressors. Jim's body now seemed 10 times more sensitive to stress than in the past, and even a small nuisance induced a stress response. He once told her he felt like a bruised fighter who had been repeatedly knocked down in a boxing match, but he wasn't giving up. He also liked talking to the nutritionist who suggested vitamins and supplements; but Jim was growing tired of the 25 different pills he had to ingest every day. Jim's appetite was poor, so the vitamins probably took up more space in his stomach than the food. When his nutritionist sent Jim some articles suggesting that schizophrenia could be cured by megadoses of vitamins, Jim began to doubt his claims altogether.

Jim hired a cook to prepare more balanced and nutritious meals than he could manage. The macrobiotic cook was a young woman who had been trained in many areas of Eastern medicine and who was studying to be a chiropractor. For six months, she cooked in Jim's kitchen for two afternoons each week. She was one of Jim's few regular contacts during that time. As she busied herself quietly in the kitchen, she never missed an opportunity to gently encourage Jim. She was confident he would heal over time. Jim found little notes scribbled on the back of his cancelled checks: "Peace," "Love to all," "Joy to life."

With the small gifts of the commonplace came other helpful images. Closing his eyes, Jim saw himself moving down a long tunnel of light and crossing a membrane to a space where everything was beautiful and peaceful. There was no more stress, and Jim felt a certain detachment and a loving affection for everything in the world. As Jim weakened, the vision grew stronger. There was a tension between what he wanted to be and how difficult it was for him to cope with day-to-day tasks.

Since his return from the CFS clinic, Jim had done everything he could think of to get better. He had always been so successful in solving his own problems, that he was sure he would find a solution for himself. He was indeed adept at organizing his own treatment plan. Various friends visited him at home to give him polarity massages and teach him self-hypnosis. His cook prepared nutritious meals. He used biofeedback to warm the temperature of his fingers and checked on his blood pressure to reduce high levels of stress. He meditated and tried to relax each day. In spite of what he referred to as "comprehensive strategies," his health continued to crumble. The burden of his illness had filled Jim's horizon with a private preoccupation that left little room for anyone else. Jim understood enough about the immune system to know that the hopelessness that came with solitude was not helpful.

A Little Help from My Friends

As Jim tried to think of ways to end his isolation, two of his dearest friends invited him to stay at their house. It took repeated invitations to convince Jim, but he finally agreed to stay with Karen and Mike for a couple of days. The place—an airy prairie-style house—was just what Jim needed. At first, Jim just explored room after room, discovering an eclectic mix of furniture, rugs, collections of art objects, and sagging bookcases. There were a lot of books and tapes on esoteric subjects that were unknown to Jim. Each object in the house looked like it had been carefully chosen by Karen and Mike. There was a relationship between the space and everything in it that fed Jim with a new sense of energy. The backyard was a Zenlike composition of carefully manicured lawn, rocks, and ancient trees, where Jim sat for hours, lost in reverie.

Karen and Mike were good cooks and even better conversationalists. Jim thrived on the lovingly cooked meals and the heartwarming conviviality. Jim was starting to wish that he could extend his stay when Karen learned her father had just been diagnosed with cancer. Under the circumstances, Jim knew not to overstay his welcome. Karen and Mike needed privacy to attend to the crisis. Besides, Jim's experience was sufficient to prove to him that he needed to be in a healing community. Both the CFS clinic on the East Coast and his stay with Karen and Mike had given him a taste of how he might get well.

Emboldened by this new knowledge, Jim flew to Montana a few months later for a 10-day stay with a few friends he had made in the CFS clinic. Jim knew Montana was famous for its pristine expanses of wild land, but what he saw still took his breath away. His friends Robert and Rebecca had a ranch where they raised sheep, bred horses, and grew organic crops. The place was limited to a house and stables, but the way the small compound was nestled in the pines on the side of a mountain made it unique.

The first evening, Rebecca hosted several friends of hers, all women, who had come to participate in what Rebecca called a healing circle.

As Jim was introduced, Rebecca explained the purpose of their meeting. Rebecca met with this group of women every two weeks to provide support and nurturing for all members of the group. The women seemed connected by a common yearning for the spiritual (there was an artist, an educator, and even a Quaker). Jim was asked to join their evening meeting, which was to last from 7 to 10 P.M. Jim accepted, feeling especially honored as the first man in the group. Rebecca had told her friends about Jim, and they were interested in meeting this strange Midwesterner.

They quietly walked into the woods above the ranch house. When they got to a clearing, they sat in a circle and absorbed the beauty of the Montana mountains as the sun disappeared behind the crest. The women took turns talking about painful and uplifting experiences they had over the last few weeks. Rebecca—the unofficial group leader—asked questions and directed the conversation when it needed to be clarified. For the first hour and a half, Jim kept quiet. Unsure of his role, he felt a little like an intruder in a women's group. Just as he wondered whether he was an observer or a participant, he was asked several questions and began talking about himself.

Jim talked haltingly at first, but he was gradually finding some sense in what he was saying. What amazed him, he went on, was how the same activity could be done in a profane or a sacred way, depending on the way it was done and the way it was thought about. It was like fasting; a few days without food or water could be healing in the context of a religious community, or it could be deadly in different circumstances. It all depended on your mindset.

A woman mentioned that birds that usually flew over this section of the mountains could not be heard that evening. Jim replied that the birds were in the trees above, listening to their conversation.

As the group ended, Rebecca and Jim lay on the ground, and the other four women placed their hands on them. After 10 minutes, Rebecca sat up to also place her hands on Jim. Jim was a little tense, amused by the oddness of the situation, but the illness had forced him to surrender prior illusions of knowledge. He was now willing to consider new things with less judgment. Jim was nevertheless very conscious of lying on the ground with the hands of five women on him.

"The heat from their hands entered my body" Jim described. "I felt very energized, almost as if I were being charged by a battery."

Jim said he felt a protective glow around his body. The mosquitoes that landed on him did not bite him. Jim said he felt protected from the external world by the healing circle that Rebecca and her friends had created.

The next day, Jim played with the two cats that lived in the ranch. They lounged around for hours, stretched in the sun, and suddenly pounced on butterflies. If only I could be more like a cat, Jim thought, I might get stronger.

Jim was introduced to another person with CFS who had just arrived at the ranch with his wife. For the next 10 days, they took time to talk around bonfires; they read; they made sculptures and masks. Jim started learning yoga and meditation, and feeling more adventurous, he took part in what was described to him as rebirthing exercises.

Jim felt so much better that he followed the group when everyone went to a secluded lake, where friends of Rebecca and Robert had lent them their house. One afternoon, as Jim was having lunch outside with everyone else, he suddenly caught himself. I feel normal, he thought. He could actually keep up with several people in a conversation without becoming exhausted. It had been so long that it seemed almost strange, like he had just been awakened from a bad dream. Lost in reflection, his gaze drifted up to a cloud of insects that were trapped in the parasol over the dinner table. The insects kept flying up and hitting the top of the large umbrella. They could have easily flown around the edge of the umbrella, but they could not see the escape route. They were trapped by their limited perception. The others at the table started looking too. As they watched these insects desperately trying to fly toward the sunlight that streamed through the transparent umbrella, Jim said, "In a sense, we are all trapped. We all have our escape routes if we could only see them. I also had an escape route, but I kept flying into an invisible net, one filled with fear, anxiety, and stress."

One evening, as Jim meditated with Rebecca and Robert, he felt a warm energy coursing through his entire body. Jim could not understand what was happening, but he sat there in a glow of energy, filled with a love toward the entire world. He went to bed knowing that he had just experienced something profound, but whatever it was kept him awake that evening.

Even this temporary community had instilled Jim with the hope he so desperately needed. He could actually be with people again, be somewhat active, and feel human again. On the last day, Robert invited Jim to stay longer, but Jim declined, afraid he might overstay

his welcome. He could always resort to this community or one like it
if his health failed again.

After visiting the East Coast CFS clinic, the home of Karen and
Mike, and the ranch in Montana, Jim had a glimpse of what healing was. It involved being with loving, caring, supportive people. He
was beginning to trust the intuition that helped him make the right
treatment decisions for himself. It was an intuition he was beginning
to think of as an inner guide. Jim would continue to listen to others
for good ideas, but true healing would most likely come from a slow
transformation and from his "daily talks with an inner healer."

Jim was now in better health after a summer of considerable healing. His food allergies had subsided; he had gained about 10 pounds;
and his stomach and intestinal problems were beginning to clear up.
He stopped needing weekly support calls to his psychotherapist, and
he was becoming less interested in the many homeopathic remedies
that his doctor was prescribing. His increasing knowledge of nutrition
showed him that the conflicting approaches to healthy eating were all
valid. Similarly, the many spiritual practices Jim had encountered had
common themes. Jim was learning to extract useful meaning from
the chaos of information at his disposal, and he was beginning to
trace his own path to health. His two principal problems now were
insomnia (it took him about an hour to fall asleep, and he often woke
up during the night) and low energy (he could be active for only a
couple of hours each day). Confident that these problems would fade
in the upcoming months, Jim decided to look for the next location to
continue his healing.

When Jim returned home, his friends Mike and Karen told him
about a Rudolph Steiner-inspired place called Camp Hill, where people with developmental disorders lived together with healthy people
in a healing community. After talking to several people who lived in
one of these communities in Minnesota, Jim found out that a couple
wanted to start a Camp Hill for people who needed to recover from
health crises. Jim was grateful for the opportunity to stay in their 300-
acre farm north of Minneapolis.

Community Living

Jim was fortunate to catch a ride to Minneapolis with a friend.
He then drove a rental car down a long dirt path that led to an old
wooden Victorian house. Nick and Cheryl appeared from behind a
hedge to greet him. They were busy harvesting a new crop of squash

from their community garden, so their sleeves were rolled up and patches of brown dirt stained their kneecaps. Here and there, cases of lettuce, carrots, and potatoes were pilling up. Nick and Cheryl practiced community-supported agriculture. City folks bought their crops before the harvest and got a delicious return on their investment when the crops reached maturity. Many of the investors also came out to the farm and helped with the harvest.

As Jim expected from people who lived so close to the land, Nick and Cheryl's spirituality was intimately connected to the bounty they received from the earth. In the two-story house, plump squash was stored here and there for the winter. They cooked hearty food, and before each meal, the family would hold hands and say a blessing, giving thanks for the food, or sing a homemade song.

"Blessings on the blossoms," they chanted. "Blessings on the fruit, blessings on the leaves and stems, blessings on the root."

Cheryl wanted to start up what she called an anthroposophic community; a place where people who were tired and depleted could heal at their own pace. In the pleasant September and October weather, Jim took day trips to nearby state parks and country towns, looked at the leaves turn, and swam in lakes. At first, he swam for a couple of minutes, and gradually worked his way up to 10 minutes, but he felt tired the next day. By the end of October, he could swim a slow breast stroke for 15 minutes in a public pool he had found. Jim was slowly getting stronger, crediting his recovery to the day trips, the excellent organic food, and the way Cheryl cooked it. To show his gratitude, Jim volunteered to wash the daily mountain of dishes. Still loyal to his old scholarly pursuits, Jim went to the local library almost every day.

He found his favorite passage in *Love, Medicine, and Miracles*, Bernie Siegel's (1990) book about Wild Bill, an inmate in a Nazi concentration camp. Wild Bill's family had been rounded up and killed, but instead of hating their killers, Wild Bill chose to love them. Even as he was surrounded by hate, Wild Bill encouraged others with his vitality, his positive and enthusiastic attitude. Jim wondered if he had the fortitude to be grateful for even the most difficult times in his life.

As he perused the library stacks, Jim also found an article by Shapiro (1989), who described Judaism as a journey of transformation. Sixteenth-century Jewish mystic Rabbi Issac Luria told of the holy sparks of God's light within everything, sparks invisible to those confused by obstacles and distractions. As he read on, Jim realized that he would need to emphasize his opening to God in order to undergo a personal transformation.

Jim had a CFS relapse in early November—along with a mild fever and a sore throat. He blamed a chill in the weather and a guest who came into the house with a cold.

Thinking that he still had more to learn, Jim started a mantralike recitation of three words: *patience, balance,* and *love.* It was difficult for Jim to accept a worsening of his CFS symptoms. In order to readjust his expectations, he needed to feel more gratitude for what little he did have. Jim had always wanted more than he'd had. If he could only accept his lot, even a tiny one, he would be on his way to recovery.

Jim's room was on the second floor, and the house had very high ceilings. He tried to cope with the falling temperatures in the drafty house by reading under a blanket. Nick and Cheryl departed for a trip to the East Coast just as snow started falling. After spending several more weeks alone in cold weather and feeling increasingly isolated, he decided to continue his recovery in warmer weather. Jim found extensive literature about the alternative communities movement on Nick and Cheryl's bookshelves. According to some of their books, there was a whole intentional communities movement around the country (see Rudee and Blease's 1989 *Traveler's Guide to Healing Centers and Retreats in North America* and McLaughlin and Davidson's 1985 *Builders of the Dawn*). Jim wrote and telephoned people at these communities to ask about staying there. Gesundheit in Virginia was a free, health-oriented community where people could recover from illness. Jim managed to reach the director only to be told that this community would not be opening for a couple of years. L'Arche was a community for people with mental retardation, similar in its mission to the Camp Hill communities and the anthroposophic movement. Unfortunately, they did not accept people who were not mentally retarded. At The Farm, none of the residents would sponsor him. The problem seemed to be that all the communities Jim contacted were looking for hard-working members who could help build their communities in concrete ways. No one would consider accepting a person as depleted as Jim.

New Age Florida

In December, in search of warm weather, Jim flew to an inexpensive resort north of Tampa. When Jim had seen its ad for a spiritual community, he had thought that the best part about it was that no work was required. He could tolerate the New Age atmosphere as long as he could stay on the two-and-a-half-acre property for the next three months and do nothing.

At the end of a long, bumpy, dirt road that wound through thick vegetation were five strange-looking buildings completely built from recyclable materials. About a mile away, a large swimming pond was filled with water that gushed from a nearby spring.

Each new place that Jim had found in his search for healing was stranger than the last one. The two owners were as unusual as the place. One was in his late fifties, a self-described disciple of Maharajii, a guru from India he had discovered after experimenting with LSD in his youth. He spent hours garbage-picking for materials that would eventually become part of the resort. The other owner was his twenty-something girlfriend, who spent part of her time cooking for the happy assembly.

Jim's cottage was furnished with an oddly painted, eclectic mix, probably the result of years of scouring nearby alleys. After unpacking his bags, Jim went outside and stood in front of his living quarters, trying to decide what he thought of the place. It was actually an old trailer that the owners had managed to drag to its permanent location. There were car parts and bicycles everywhere, nothing that worked, though. The ground was crawling with big fire ants, so Jim guessed yoga would have to take place inside the trailer. Suddenly, two armadillos burst out of the thick curtain of Spanish moss and headed straight for Jim. As suddenly as they had appeared, they stopped inches from his feet. Jim, who had never seen armadillos, stared at their prehistoric armor in disbelief. The animals stared back with their beady eyes, took a few quick steps in the dust with their stubby little legs, and trotted back into the brush. Quite a welcome! Jim thought.

Jim spent the first few days lying in a hammock he had found hanging between two trees. It kept the fire ants at bay, but Jim noticed some vultures gliding overhead. In search of carrion, the birds were probably unsure about the immobile silhouette they saw hanging between two trees. Was it still alive? Jim dozed off in the humid heat. He was awakened every now and then by a shotgun blast and a litany of curses, every time his neighbor Pluto fired his shotgun at the birds. The vultures weren't the only ones eyeing Jim. The unorthodox owners could not figure out why Jim didn't move all day. They didn't mind some of the 10 other guests who wandered half-naked throughout the resort in drug-induced psychoses, or the shotgun-wielding Pluto, but the normal-looking guy who stayed in his hammock all day was making them paranoid. Jim felt anything but normal as he slowly recovered from the fatigue, but compared to everyone else around, he definitely stood out. As he had expected, Jim regained some of his strength. Every day, he practiced 20 minutes of gentle yoga exercises in the trailer and walked or swam for a few minutes. Like before, he felt depleted for a couple of days if he pushed himself too hard. Jim noticed that when the weather was warm enough to sit outside, he generally felt better, but even in Florida, his throat continued to be sore.

One day, while Jim walked along one of the many dirt roads, a dog came racing down a long driveway, barking ferociously. The driveway was about the length of two football fields, and the dog got bigger as it got closer. Jim was tempted to run, but the dog was much quicker. Climbing a tree was out of the question. The dog was definitely big. The only solution was to show no fear. If I am friendly and loving, he thought, the dog might not attack me.

"Hi, doggy! Hello!" Jim heard himself say in a pleasant voice to the approaching hound.

The dog stopped 10 yards away and quietly looked at Jim. Immobile, it just kept staring at Jim, who started walking away. I have nothing to fear, Jim thought, noting how deeply the incident had transformed him.

One of the resort guests, a tour bus driver from Wisconsin named Christopher, claimed that he had been trained in India in different systems of healing. After striking a conversation, Christopher placed his hands in the air around Jim's arm and said Jim's energy field boundaries were more permeable than anyone he'd ever seen. Jim thought of himself as incredibly sensitive to almost everything in life, and a broken energy field was at least a plausible explanation of his extreme vulnerability.

Some of the New Age guests had a taste for the esoteric. It was tricky to distinguish valid practices out of their original context and in the midst of other questionable events. Francis and Thomas, for example, swore by the value of hypnotic age regressions; they believed they had lived many lives before. One rather flamboyant guest told Jim that she was 1,600 years old. Francis and Thomas explained what chakras were—an Indian system of energy fields—and concluded that Jim's heart chakra, which was symbolized by love, needed to be developed. Then they took LSD, and Jim watched as Francis and Thomas wandered through the resort, hallucinating. Intrigued, Jim found himself able to sustain conversations for hours with his new friends. Francis and Thomas left the resort a few days later, smothering Jim in a bear hug. Jim was a little startled, but felt loved nonetheless.

Another guest, Cathleen, had been hypnotized by Leo and had discovered several past lives. She told Jim in a serious tone that, during one of these past lives, she had been the third pope. Jim found the séances mildly entertaining, but one thing about Cathleen interested him. She described herself as a radiance healer who had cured herself of a chronic illness. During one of her radiance therapy sessions, she laid her hands on Jim's shoulders and said he was literally soaking in energy. Jim's skepticism was tempered by the fact that several practitioners had now told him that his energy field was unbalanced.

After an acupuncture massage by another guest, Jim learned how the body's energy channels had been mapped in meridians by Chinese acupuncturists. In the United States, Wilhelm Reich had experimented with healing energy within the body that he called orgone. In India, prana, or life energy, had been mapped out into the body's energy centers, or chakras. In Western religions life energy had also been referred to as the Holy Spirit by biblical prophets.

During one evening's guided imagery session, Jim was asked to picture the brain as two sides divided by an alley. He pictured three doors labeled fear, desire, and ego on the left side, and three doors labeled patience, balance, and love on the right side. Jim pictured himself entering the patience room, only to find a large hole in the floor. Jim interpreted this to mean that he needed to let go of certain things and to fall below the realm of ordinary life before he could heal.

After three months, Jim was ready to go home. On his last 20-minute walk, a large dog jumped out of the bushes and started running down the road toward Jim. It was a different dog than the one he had seen a few weeks before; it was at least twice as large. It must have weighed over 200 pounds. Carried by its momentum, the dog overshot Jim, narrowly missing his leg. The dog swung around and lunged forward with a gaping mouthful of yellow teeth. Jim kept walking, and the dog missed again. Jim knew he would survive. Confidently, he told himself he needed to overcome this frightening and threatening situation. "You are my friend," he said, looking directly at the dog. The dog stopped growling and looked at Jim with puzzlement. Jim had met the challenge with grace and fortitude.

Jim related feeling much stronger from his journey. He had passed through several supportive communities where loving people made attempts at healing him. This made him feel protected. As Jim returned home, he wondered how much of this would stay with him.

Coming Home

Jim had come home during the warmer spring days, so he often spent the afternoons sitting on the fire escape outside his condominium. He had transformed a small area into his sacred space, from which he gazed at the now-familiar view. From his old chair with chipping black paint, he could see the alley below, the brown building across, and above it the sky and a few treetops. At the end of the alley, he saw a few feet of pavement, and occasionally people walking by. The alley people were most interesting, the ones who rummaged through the garbage, looking for recyclables and things they could use. Jim only moved his chair to let an occasional neighbor through. He didn't care what they thought of this man who stared out into the alley all day.

Jim thought of himself as the guardian of the alley. Hardly an hour passed without a squirrel running across the telephone line with something in its mouth. The clouds formed interesting shapes in the narrow rectangle of sky. He kept track of the birds, the butterflies, and the occasional wandering pet. He listened to the sound of the wind in the phone lines, and he watched the weeds grow through the cracks in the pavement.

With hindsight, Jim realized that these peaceful moments were propitious for healing. It was then that he began to mend and regain his energy.

Having regained enough strength, Jim returned to his former job on a part-time basis. He functioned with a little more than half the energy he previously had, but this was a vast improvement. Over the next 10 years, Jim's health gradually improved. His supportive work environment, where he was able to gradually increase his workload, was an important part of his recovery, as well as his efforts to find healing within communities.

Lessons Learned

The lack of affordable housing is usually a complicating factor that causes the health of people with CFS and other chronic health conditions to further deteriorate. As a result, some people with CFS are homeless, and others are so desperate that they have contacted Dr. Kervorkian to end their lives. Suicide and other unfortunate ends might be prevented if affordable housing and support were available.

Jim's path to recovery from CFS involved searching for a loving, protective community he was able to find first with friends, and then in several other small communities. Along the way, Jim discovered what specifically would help him recover. Those with chronic illnesses need these types of protective settings. Jim was fortunate to have the financial resources to design himself a support network, where he could successively tap into one community after another until he regained enough strength to sustain himself. Unfortunately, many CFS patients don't have such resources, or may not find communities that meet their individual needs. There is a dire need for communities designed specifically for people with debilitating chronic medical illnesses like CFS.

Once his illness began, Jim slowly realized how concretely problematic his work habits had been. He attributed part of the breakdown to his perfectionist race for professional honors and his overachieving ideals. The paradox, it seemed to him, was that he worked so hard in the hope of reaching some sort of invincibility, and that it ultimately caused him to become extremely vulnerable.

Jim had come a long way from his secular, atheistic world. His journey had begun with a challenge to God. He had rejected his religion because he refused to practice customs that were based on historical events that seemed violent and sexist. Yet he now realized that all religions had practices that might seem absurd from a contemporary perspective. His challenge was to translate ancient images into relevant symbols for the twenty-first century. By losing everything, he had begun to better appreciate the small daily miracles that were right in front of him. Instead of finding the terror and suffering of the world so draining, he could even feel compassion and empathy for it, with a little distance. Most importantly, Jim felt he had gained new insight into the healing process: there were no universal formulas; each person had to find the unique catalysts to his or her recovery.

Mostly, the work he did in the communities he inhabited consisted of making relationships with other people, with the world around him, and with a spiritual realm of his choosing. Mutual and deep relating required Jim to gradually transcend his ego, a process that surrendering to the illness had already initiated. As he opened his heart to others, to animals, plants, and even to things he previously thought of as inanimate, Jim gained a sense of oneness with the universe. Wherever he stood in the world, he felt he belonged, and he was grateful for that.

Angela's Battle

After he returned home, Jim made a point of nurturing friendships, even if he only had a few minutes of precious energy to spare
on some days. Coincidentally, one of the people he met at that time
told Jim that she had been sick with CFS since 1982. Angela did test
positive for mononucleosis; she suffered from an old back injury she
sustained while she moved a piano; and she was coming out of an
abusive marriage with an alcoholic husband, but neither a single one
of these biographical tidbits nor their combination sufficed to explain
how she had gotten so sick. Her life story was offered to Jim in way of
self-introduction as much as speculation on the etiology of what she
now knew to be CFS.

The trajectory of Angela's career is a good indication of the impact
this illness has on productive lives. With her master's degree in
human resource management, she went from raising funds and managing the accreditation of a large community mental health center
to teaching court reporting and business courses. Her next career
move took her to helping create a school for Hispanic students. She
routinely interfaced with several people at once, showing both facility
and vitality in her work.

That changed after the Memorial Day weekend of 1982, when
Angela felt sharp pains in her joints, particularly in her hands. She
woke up the next day with what felt like the worst flu she'd ever had.
The joint pain made sleeping difficult, and she felt nauseated, but an
unnerving weakness forced her to stay in bed. After a week off work
did no good, Angela asked a friend to drive her to an internist, who
hospitalized her for a week to test her for rheumatoid arthritis, among
other things.

Bolstered by negative results on all the tests, Angela talked herself
back to work, where she oversaw night school from 2 P.M. to 10 P.M.
With hindsight, she estimated that she was able to use only 50 percent
of her prior energy and mental acuity. Even a new, less-demanding
job (35 hours a week) left her depleted. Thanks to supportive colleagues, she was able to hang on to her job for three more years. That
was when she was diagnosed with mononucleosis.

Exhausted, Angela resigned herself to moving back in with her
mother, where she spent three months in bed. Once she managed to
get up, she took a full-time secretarial job. She made it through the
day by eating Oreo cookies, and she crashed on her bed when she got
home at night. Determined to get better, Angela enrolled the help

of a former student to move into an apartment. By 1991, breathing difficulties started, joint pain got worse, and Angela felt her intellect slipping. Having lost her job, she survived on a monthly pittance of $152 from public aid and $70 in food stamps. She lay in bed, knocked down by her symptoms, watching her meager resources dwindle. When she managed to reach someone in social services on the phone, she could not even articulate her request. She was too tired to make a compelling case for herself on the phone, and the social worker on the other end dismissed her request. In theory at least, any human service professional should be at least a little inquisitive when someone makes an unclear or unconvincing request on the phone. After all, people in need tend to find their life depressing, which doesn't help to make them assertive. In Angela's case, though, the call did not help.

After living for six months in her apartment, Angela realized that it had been repainted before she moved in and that the kitchen cabinets and carpets had been replaced. A little research showed her that brand new materials were installed before they cured correctly, and they possibly emitted substantial amounts of formaldehyde gas. Empowered by the discovery that she might be suffering from multiple chemical sensitivity (MCS) as well as mononucleosis and CFS, Angela moved to a new, safer apartment.

The clean air in her new place allowed Angela to feel better. She obtained Social Security benefits and felt financially stable for the first time in six months. She dated a man for a while, but couldn't keep up with the social demands of dating. Angela was feeling vulnerable already, so when he broke it off, she did not take it well. Angela went to bed that night after she swallowed a whole bottle of Klonopin, but she woke up, still very much alive, and called 911.

During the two weeks she spent on a psychiatry ward for attempting to take her own life, Angela found only one nurse who showed sympathy and made allowances for her CFS symptoms. Everyone else bullied her out of bed, told her to be more independent, and generally treated her depression as a primary problem. No one there could understand that her suicidal feelings were secondary to a syndrome that made her life miserable. Naturally, Angela felt like this treatment was not for her, as it failed to address the fundamental reasons for her suffering.

Out of the hospital, Angela fumed over the system that had victimized her and insensitive professionals who ignored everything about CFS. Maybe her anger could fuel her efforts to help others in a similar quandary. After meeting with other CFS patients in a local support group, she began listing resources for people with disabilities, and she used her own phone to create a homemade CFS hotline. Some people called regularly and became friendlier with every call. She walked them through the application for Social Security disability benefits, and turned them on to meals on wheels and homemaker services. "A stranger is just a friend I haven't met yet," Angela remembered thinking as she witnessed her own support network develop.

After a few years, Angela accepted the office of president of the CFS support group. In addition to what she was already doing, she held group meetings at her apartment. Seeing the big picture of the group and the alienation still experienced by its members made Angela realize that something more comprehensive needed to be done. The quality of life of CFS sufferers was lowest among anyone with a disability. This was due in part to the failure of social service agencies to recognize the syndrome, thereby denying services and housing, but also to the plethora of viral and somatic complaints. People with CFS needed a genuine community based on specialized housing. A group in California, Ecology House, had successfully built such a community.

Ecology House was an 11-unit apartment complex in San Rafael, California, that affordably housed persons with MCS—an illness triggered by exposure to various chemicals like perfumes or petroleum products. It attracted national media attention as the first apartment building in the United States constructed and maintained with materials that were safer for persons with MCS. Through the 811 Housing and Urban Development (HUD) program, an organization could be funded to buy property and renovate it or construct new housing. Subsidies from this HUD program also limited rent to 30 percent of occupants' adjusted gross income, provided residents with rides to buy groceries or get to medical appointments, and paid for a cook. Knowing that the government distributed hundreds of millions of dollars each year for these types of housing initiatives, Angela began putting together an 811 housing application for people with CFS. Had she foreseen where such a clear request was about to take her, she might have gotten discouraged.

In December 2000, Angela formed a CFS housing committee and met with a HUD official. A few requirements emerged from this meeting. The committee needed to hire a consultant to write the grant ($10,000), have control (possession) of the land, pay $20,000 for an environmental site assessment, and pay $10,000 as a minimal capital investment (i.e., to pay for control over the land). Despite this imposing laundry list, the HUD official was optimistic; he knew the housing commissioner and felt this was a worthy cause.

Angela found a consultant who was willing to be paid only when the grant was submitted. The consultant added another requirement to the already long list: an umbrella agency needed to submit the grant to assuage the fears of HUD funders that the homegrown CFS support group was not qualified to manage a comprehensive housing project. Lutheran Social Services was identified as a likely candidate and agreed to submit the 811 application on the group's behalf. A not-for-profit board was established to manage the future building, with CFS group constituents as board members. With all its ducks in a row, the board had every reason to be confident as it set out on a search for adequate land. There were several buildings in need of renovation, but the cost of refurbishing was rendered prohibitive by American with Disabilities Act housing standards. Demolition was not covered by the HUD grant, and there too, the cost of hazardous materials abatement (at issue in all buildings built before 1972) was astronomical. Vacant land was decidedly the only option, but most empty lots in the city were already zoned for commercial use, and they sold faster than anyone tied to a grant schedule could hope to buy them. The commissioner of housing offered the possibility of using land empowerment zones, but the housing consultant reminded the board that HUD was unlikely to grant money for housing in high-crime areas where people with disabilities could not be reasonably safe. Other grants wouldn't help: a capacity building grant was limited to $5,000. A predevelopment loan wouldn't be available until after the grant application deadline because it had to be approved by the city council. In a short time, Angela's optimism had been buried under a mountain of red tape.

Disappointed, the group looked at its options. An alderman and the city planning department suggested the rather aggressive strategy of targeting TIF districts, which basically consisted of claiming control over a problematic building (likely a transient hotel used for drugs and prostitution). The city would draft the document making the power transfer official, only too happy to find someone who would push out undesirable elements, then would watch as the hotel owner and the CFS group duked it out in court. Notwithstanding the glum prospect of being sued for loss of business and the possibility of paying well over the market value for the building if they won the case, the CFS group had moral reservations about what amounted to an opportunistic, if not predatory, move. Besides, the riddle of the high cost of renovation or demolition was still unsolved.

Two months before the grant application deadline, in a last-ditch effort, the group contacted a real estate agent who owned suburban land parcels zoned commercial for the first floor, but above which residences could be built. The agent planned on selling 10 to 15 units to HUD; the CFS group would save $10,000 for site control and $20,000 for an environmental site assessment. The group would only have to pay $10,000 to the consultant. Even the HUD official like the idea, but upon checking with his legal department, he turned it down. The building had to be already built and inspected by HUD before a grant could be funded. Even after the building was built and inspected, the developer could not get paid for a year, the time it would take for funds to be disbursed. Not even the most well-meaning developer could wait a year between the sale contract and the closing.

Finally, another false hope was dashed when plans with another agency fell through. The agency could write the grant to build on land it already owned. It was the best solution that presented itself so far, but the agency pulled out.

As the grant application deadline passed, Angela and the CFS group finally understood why 811 grants were written by large not-for-profit organizations. The costs of the application process alone were overwhelming. For over six months, the group had jumped through hoop after hoop in an adversarial, dog-eat-dog world. No allowances were made for group members' reduced ability to endure this battle. It seemed impossible to compete in a volatile real estate market, where deals were struck in a matter of hours, when the CFS group was bound by rigid governmental regulations and slow-moving bureaucracy.

Angela tried to secure government funds to create a housing community for people with CFS. We will explore some of the challenges of depending on government finances to create these types of communities in the next chapter. Certainly, the experience of community members in Oxford Houses suggests that there are alternative approaches to creating low-cost housing. Angela continues to work with a group of volunteers on this housing project. She does not think she has failed, but only has been delayed from reaching her ultimate goal: the creation of a vibrant and meaningful home where people with CFS can find respect and hope.

CHAPTER 6

OTHER HAVENS

There are too many worthwhile communities to mention in these pages, but we felt we should at least mention a few more that already exist for people who suffer from a variety of conditions. Ordinary citizens have taken extraordinary steps to develop communities that offer companionship, friendship, and support in bearing the burden of day-to-day living (Fellowship for Intentional Community, 1990). For example, in 1964 Jean Vanier, a philosopher, founded l'Arche, a community where people with mental retardation and fully developed intelligence lived together. Vanier had little formal knowledge of mental retardation; therefore, his approach had more to do with a philosophy of respect for human dignity than with the expectations that human service professionals usually bring to housing initiatives. At l'Arche, the humanizing lifestyle follows a pattern of work (gardening, housekeeping, or workshop), meals, and recreation. At the heart of the community, members struggle to grow in "their capacity to be more open and loving within the ideals of communitarianism" (Dunne, 1986, p. 47). Dunne further suggests that the sense of community, as experienced at l'Arche, is "an awareness of the relationships and accepting the risks, pain, and weaknesses encountered in self and others" (p. 53). In the years since the project's inception, more than 70 l'Arche communities have been formed.

There are other examples of ordinary citizens acting on the realization that the elderly and people with disabilities often need support that is not readily available from the family or society. One such individual is Bill Allison, founder of the Needs Foundation. Bill's wife suffered from multiple sclerosis (MS), and Bill and his wife needed more in-home support than their income and insurance allowed. Bill recognized that his family was not the only one faced with the need for affordable in-home assistance. While watching a television documentary highlighting the plight of the homeless, it occurred to Bill that there were probably homeless people who could be trained to provide nonmedical in-home care. Ideally, such an arrangement would benefit both individuals. The elderly person or the person with a disability would receive affordable assistance, while the caregiver would acquire training, an alternative living arrangement, and work experience. The Needs Foundation facilitates the matching of care receivers and caregivers through an extensive screening and matching process. To date, more than 100 matches have been arranged (Ogintez, 1992). The individuals involved in these relationships find a sense of connection and community (Ferrari, Billows, & Jason, 1997).

Another group that has been involved in establishing housing and communities for its members is Multiple Sclerosis People Helping People. This not-for-profit organization's sole purpose is to create and operate independent housing for anyone with MS (their Web site can be accessed at http://www.msphp.org). MS patients have very energetic brains with high intelligence, but their bodies have begun to fail. When this occurs, they live in nursing homes or at home, alone and unattended, which sometimes leads them to seek assisted suicide (the majority of patients who have sought assisted suicide had MS). A patient of Dr. Prasad in Indiana had lost 200 pounds, developing sepsis (a kind of generalized infection) and bone marrow depression, with skin sloughing on her bones. As this patient began to recover, Dr. Prasad offered her own second home as housing, but she feared the patient could not handle living there alone. Dr. Prasad invited two other patients to move in as well. One of them had been stuck in a nursing home, which was making her depressed. Once this small community was created, these three lives improved dramatically. The patient who was near death has gone shopping and visited an invalid son. Another, who had been wheelchair-bound, is now not only able to stand but can also dance.

Adelman and Frey (1994) have described a unique residential facility in Chicago. This setting houses 30 men and women with HIV, many of whom already show symptoms of AIDS. Founded in 1988 by the Alexian Brothers, a Roman Catholic community of men, Bonaventure House is a vital community of people with HIV/AIDS. Residents have reported that the opportunity for increased social support was one of their most important reasons for moving into Bonaventure House.

The Alexian Brothers who live in this house are paid a minimum salary and are perceived as figures of great compassion. A paid staff member is available to help in navigating through the maze of social services. Volunteers are also available, offering practical, emotional, and social support. What distinguishes Bonaventure House from the other communities is that the residents are living with the reality of their own death and of the deaths of the people with whom they have formed relationships. Group rituals have emerged to deal with the grieving process. For example, there is a balloon-releasing ceremony that functions as a symbolic letting-go of a resident who has died.

Fairweather (1979) developed another haven called the Lodge that was specifically designed for individuals with serious mental disorders. The Lodge was created as a self-governing organization, thereby allowing its members participative roles in management and decision making. Professionals could thus assume the role of consultant. This therefore allowed them to play a meaningful part in the creation of the organization without taking it over. As a further part of the program, members owned and operated their own business. This allowed members the opportunity to assume productive work roles. The program was not designed to be transitional, but rather to function as a surrogate family for members (Tornatzky & Fergus, 1982). Lodges have now been established throughout the United States, and a group called the National Conference of Adopters Coalition for Community Living currently serves to unite Lodge adopters.

Health care providers have developed a number of innovative models for helping patients with serious mental illness. Many attempt to create havens in their own homes and neighborhoods. One example is Assertive Community Treatment, whose teams provide case management, initial and ongoing assessments, psychiatric services, employment and housing assistance, family support and education, substance abuse services, and other services and supports that help individuals live successfully in the community (Bond, McDonel, & Miller, 1991; Essock, Frisman, & Kontos, 1998). Assertive Community Treatment teams also provide long-term services that involve the client's family as well as vocational rehabilitation services and community employment in order to further integrate patients into the community.

On Spirituality

Community building does not necessarily involve large groups of people, nor does it have to include housing initiatives. Similarly, spirituality does not need to be forced onto a community to make it successful, but it is likely that the sharing of common values and traditions—usually born out of everyday necessity—will facilitate long-term cohesion. Often the experience of success and happiness through the application of these traditions will elevate them to a quasi-spiritual status. For that reason, even if a community is not centered around a spiritual practice, its members will end up feeling like they are part of something greater than themselves.

During the interviews we conducted with community members, we noticed the high quality of their presence. The quality of the attention they gave to us was often better than we had encountered among people in the world at large, and it was remarkable for people who were weighed down by severe disabilities. Unlike the usual definition of a participant as someone active, not passive, their full participation was qualified by the quality of their attention. The community members we saw before or after we conducted our interviews also seemed to value each other in a way that did not rest on the usual conditions of social status. They did not judge each other by what they had *become*. They knew they were no longer part of the American frenzy for overachievement—no curriculum vitae could describe their successes. They valued each other for just *being* there, which gave them a much keener appreciation for each others' unique and lovable quirks. They knew they were characters, as sympathetic as the ones in a good story. Their lives together took on a quasi-mythical and storied quality, complete with the unforeseen plot twists they seemed to now accept more easily. The narratives born in the community meetings were almost mythical, in that they dealt with the past of the group and created its future in a way that transcended individuals and relationships between them. The regularly occurring meetings took on a ritualistic quality that in turn created a sense of community. For members—whose lives had previously been so disappointing—the renewal of the greater good of the community was hard to believe, but nevertheless real. Members knew how fragile life could be, and they held up their communal success one day at a time, like a venerable mystery.

Participatory Action Research

Mainstream research in social sciences and psychology has tended to be quantitative, with an objective, controlling, and distant involvement of researchers. This traditional role has called for controlling participants, so that researchers alone define the problem to be analyzed. Traditional research subjects have been denied access to the interpretation of the data and the design of methods, despite the obvious authority they had derived from their life experience. Publications of results have not been shared with participants either. Mainstream research on addiction, which has frequently involved disenfranchised people, has often been perceived as colonizing and degrading.

Alaska Native community members who attended a 1994 National Institutes of Health conference on alcoholism in Anchorage found the focus of the presentations to be one-sided, overwhelmingly negative, discouraging, and offensive to their sense of self-worth. The dominant narrative of the two-day conference was that all Native people who drink are alcoholics, and that recovery is rare (Mohatt et al., 2001). Presenters used an oversimplified genetic explanation to demonstrate that alcohol abuse was inevitable among American Indians. No mention was made of the large numbers of American Indian people who had recovered from alcoholism, or the many who could drink socially without experiencing any harm. In this example, mainstream research proved to be of little help to the communities studied. A community leader in the audience who had been sober for years said that the conference made her feel like "going out and getting drunk." People felt that their achievements were not recognized, their voices unheard, and the results of no practical use to their struggle for sobriety.

The conflict that arose between presenters, community leaders, and academics caused a new research model to be utilized. After the conference, researchers who approached Native community leaders to invite them into a study were rebuffed unceremoniously. It was obvious that very little trust had survived from previous experiences with research projects. That trust was earned back during many months of defining dialogue with the Native community. A new method of research needed to be used, and it was called participatory action research (PAR) (Chesler, 1991). In this new paradigm, researchers and participants collaborated to define the scope of the inquiry in a way that respected the traditions of the people being studied. This synergy yielded more qualitative results, narratives that revealed themes in their rightful context. Researchers submitted results to participants, whose feedback helped to further design the study. Participants became coresearchers who shared the ownership of the data—and the rights to interpret it—with the researchers (Hazel & Mohatt, 2001).

The participatory action research that followed the Anchorage conference revealed that people needed research that helped them articulate the story of their recovery, sort of like what a book like this one could do for a community like Oxford House (communal homes where former drug and alcohol abusers recover). The qualitative narrative that emerged from participatory action research and similar forms of community psychology research emphasized what empowered people to stay sober. In other words, it raised social consciousness.

We realized that we favored the participatory action research model because we understood that a web of life connected the inhabitants of the world. Participatory approaches engage all participants as active partners in the creation and evaluation of interventions. One of the fundamental aspects of participatory research is to involve community members in an egalitarian partnership with researchers, and to empower people with the means to take control of their own lives (Jason et al., 2004). Another aspect of participatory action research is the ecological model, which provides a guiding framework for understanding behavior in interaction with its social and cultural contexts. The community psychologist Jim Kelly suggested that a fundamental principle in ecological approaches was the need to use multiple methods to understand the complex qualities of relationships and systems (Kingry-Westergaard & Kelly, 1990). The ecological model is conducive to the understanding of social phenomena (in this case, the plight of people with addictions or mental illness, the elderly, and people with chronic health problems) because of its emphasis on the collaborative relationship between researcher and participants. In such a relationship, concepts and hypotheses are developed and tested jointly by the investigator and the participants. Feminist researchers agree with this feature of the ecological model in their recommendation that we listen to and understand people first and foremost from their points of view. People involved in qualitative research projects should be participants, not subjects, and the process of being understood and represented should be considered empowering.

We understood that professionals who join in long-term collaborative relationships with individuals and groups can use ecological principles (Burgoyne & Jason, 1991; Kingry-Westergaard & Kelly, 1990). An ecological approach analyzes community traditions for responding to community problems, helps evaluate or create settings that provide individuals with opportunities to continue receiving support after the termination of formal programs, works closely with community leaders in all aspects of health care intervention, and assesses positive and negative effects of intervention.

By being actively involved in the planning of intervention programs, the recipients gain support, learn to identify resources, and
become better problem-solvers who are more likely to manage future
challenges. Collaborative interventions are more likely to have enduring results. This way, we would not only gather the information we
needed to write our book, but the information-gathering process itself
would prove to be helpful to the people we were researching.

How to Approach True Community

That sense of community can often only be found in temporary
networks, with limited support, and shifting associations. Change is
inevitable, so we must train ourselves to recognize community when
we catch a glimpse of it, and to foster its fleeting, yet vital quality.
We are not suggesting that any success can be made to last forever,
but simply that it needs to be acknowledged while it lasts, and that
any member of society can benefit greatly by being a supportive participant. The transaction between the characteristics of a person and
the environment described by psychologist Jim Kelly (1985) is at the
heart of community healing. Communities can be found that offer the
right fit for almost anyone who is looking for this kind of environmental support.

The rarity of community healing in Western society also shows
how much we discount the influence of environment on disease. If
the right kind of environment can foster healing, the wrong kind can
worsen illness. Proponents of this view tend to be patients. Part of
the reason many doctors have opposed the view that environment
had a strong bearing on health was that the medical model tradition-
ally located causes for illness within the body. While environmental
causes for physical illness are increasingly recognized, psychiatry and
psychology are also beginning to reach similar conclusions through
specialties like community psychology. Most traditional psychia-
trists would view an addict's tendency to blame external causes for
addiction as mere defensive denial, but the Oxford House experience
suggests that environment may in fact be to blame for the addiction
relapse. People with addictions found a durable and efficient road
to sobriety all by themselves by recreating their own world. Why
not use this finding to revise the way addiction treatment is being
delivered? Is the medical establishment so self-satisfied that it cannot
fathom the possibility of valuable information coming from patients
themselves?

Of course, no lessons can be learned without the willingness to just listen. Researchers, too busy establishing their own agendas, have often failed to do just that. The Oxford House chapter benefited from full-fledged research, which was conducted in keeping with the principles of participatory action research outlined in this chapter. Lines of communication were already open, and trust had been earned with Oxford House. This made the writing of the Oxford House chapter easier.

The research did not become participatory overnight, and a close look at this gradual process proved enlightening. From the time founder Paul Molloy supported the idea of DePaul University research in 1991, the research team's primary concern was to approach the Illinois members of Oxford House with respect. Early on, researchers realized that due to the innovative nature of Oxford House, they would be presented with situations unknown in more controlled studies. This sometimes required a creative revision of their roles, from researchers to advocates, consultants, or helping hands, as situations evolved.

One such situation occurred in 1992, after the administrators at the Illinois Department of Drug and Alcohol Abuse recognized the potential of Oxford House and funded a recruiter to come to Illinois to start up Oxford Houses. When the representative chosen by Molloy arrived in Chicago to open the first home, funding delays caused his housing to fall through. With nowhere else to stay, he was forced to sleep in a shelter, where all his belongings were stolen. Discouraged, the representative contemplated leaving Chicago. The man whose mission was to introduce Oxford House to Chicago was in need of help, and the DePaul researchers had to think quickly and carefully. A detached stance would prohibit them from interfering with the natural processes at work, and it would probably cause the representative to abandon the whole task. The man would probably experience it as a personal failure and relapse on drugs and alcohol. The traditional stance of objectivity, detachment, and control is achieved by excluding research subjects from knowledge of the research and by avoiding altering the field of inquiry. This stance, although it is in line with more traditional research methods, would help neither Oxford House nor the researchers. In contrast, a participatory action approach would benefit both. Researchers delineated boundaries with the Oxford House representative, defined a reciprocal relationship by creating mutual criteria, and obtained a shared agenda that would benefit both. It meant that the research team offered the representative free accommodations, first at a researcher's home, then at the DePaul Seminary. The researchers also provided him with office space, a telephone, and other resources so that he could make the necessary arrangements to establish the first Oxford House in Chicago. Because of this help, the representative called the first Illinois Oxford House the DePaul house. This episode was brought up by Oxford House members later on to let others know that the DePaul research team members could be trusted.

During the first year, one member of the research team was assigned to each house, to visit it once a month and to get to know the residents. Rather than immediately collecting data, researchers wanted to get to know the residents on a more personal level. In addition, a member of the Oxford House community attended the weekly research meetings at DePaul University and recorded these meetings to share the information with the Oxford House community. Mutual trust grew as our two groups met and learned about each other.

When the first Illinois Oxford Houses opened in 1992, the DePaul University team interviewed Oxford House members and attended monthly house meetings for 18 months (Jason, Ferrari et al., 1997). Oxford House members reported their the primary reasons for joining were (1) a sense of fellowship with other alcoholics, (2) the enforcement of set rules on sobriety, resulting in a stable environment, (3) participation in self-governing, and (4) being able to explore their own psyches without deadlines, while sober. Members also mentioned that these aspects of Oxford House were not found in other recovery programs. The research team also noted that the average weekly rent for Illinois Oxford Houses was $70 per resident, suggesting the cost-effectiveness of this approach compared to other treatment modalities, which have per-client costs ranging from $36 to $585 per day.

The DePaul team also extended support by writing proposals and grants to the Chicago Community Trust that were used to open new Oxford Houses in the Chicago area. Some of these grants were used to open homes for recovering women with young children. With grant funding, Oxford House members and the DePaul research team jointly trained and monitored a recruiter to recognize the special needs of mothers and children in the context of communal life.

Once Oxford House traditions and expectations were defined to the researchers, they set out to design a participant action research method that respected them. A few Oxford House members were offered jobs by the university as research associates. These positions strengthened the collaboration by providing members with rewarding employment, established a way for the university to administer research questionnaires, and created a climate of mutual trust. During the workday, normal interactions with research associates created a narrative, the story of life at Oxford House. As researchers and participants experienced each others' humanity, they began to gradually understand what made the Oxford House community work so well.

When the DePaul team attended the annual Oxford House convention, members were asked if there were areas that the team had omitted and needed to include in the research. An Oxford House member approached and pointed to a woman.

"See that woman; she has HIV," he said. "Before I entered Oxford House for my drug problems, I was so prejudiced I would have never even talked to her! After being in Oxford House, I learned to become more tolerant and accepting of others. Now that woman with HIV is my girlfriend." The man paused to gauge the reaction his revelation had caused, then he resumed. "In your research, you need to study how people become more tolerant. I think it's one of the most important changes inside of us."

In the following weeks, the research team created a way to measure tolerance and began including it in its interactions with Oxford House residents.

Collaborative research, like the research described throughout this book, can create work with self-help organizations that is mutually rewarding, so that the needs of both parties are met, and so that both learn from each other and become invested in the relationship. When we collaborate with community groups, we become a more caring and humane society with the means to provide decent living conditions for all our citizens. We live in an interconnected world, where the suffering of one person or one group hurts everyone else, so by helping those in need we also help ourselves. Readers who want more information on participatory action research should read Appendix G for another example of this approach with CFS.

The Effect of Government Regulations

In theory, health care regulations serve a vital purpose by protecting vulnerable patients. Horror stories about malpractice and neglect in health care institutions are so numerous in the media that they have become common currency. Although regulations makes sense from this point of view, they can be counterproductive for the communities described in this book. True community only happens with time, but the more organized and successful a community becomes, the more likely it is to come under government scrutiny. Many communities that formed organically are eventually subject to government regulation because they are seen as part of the health care system they were trying to escape in the first place. Many individuals or groups of people who can claim to have found healing through a specific set of actions or circumstances, and who endeavor to reproduce the experience in an organized fashion, are confronted with health care regulation sooner or later.

It seems unfair that people who are trying to create communal alternatives to dehumanizing institutional milieus are thwarted by the same regulations that failed to protect them when they were seeking care from institutional programs. It seems especially unjust, since most of the public funding goes to institutional programs that are not real communities. If small grassroots communities are going to be held to the same standards as huge institutions, they should at least be afforded equitable funding opportunities.

True communities cost less, but that doesn't mean that they should get less funding, proportionally, than institutional programs; it just means that they will make more efficient use of taxpayers' money. Communities for people who are unable to work need reliable funding sources, including federal grants. GROW is a good example of what federal and state funding can do in terms of reducing mental illness relapses that lead to expensive hospitalizations paid for by public funds.

At the same time, the example of GROW illustrated the inhibiting influence state regulatory agencies can have on a thriving community. GROW had succeeded in facilitating the natural phenomenon of making relationships among people whose relational capacity had been greatly reduced by mental illness. The state essentially wanted to pigeonhole nature into its little, neatly controlled categories. Fortunately, the GROW staff was able to react in a way that pleased the state and protected the health of the community.

Many other communities were not able to maintain themselves under regulatory scrutiny. An entire communal village in Oregon, where elderly people aged gracefully together, was evicted by state regulators who deemed its modest housing inadequate. All residents were forcibly relocated to nursing homes, where many soon died (Kevin McIlvoy, personal communication, August 29, 2002). It seems that, in the United States, we have a way of establishing something worthwhile, destroying it with regulations, and leaving people with only an illusion.

The people of Oxford House, GROW, and H.O.M.E. were part of real communal life, not illusions of communities. The chapter on CFS and other chronic medical ailments described a failed attempt to create community, but it also showed that even the effort of looking for peer support can be empowering. It is impossible to name all the community housing initiatives for people with chronic health challenges in the United States, but we believe that identifying a few communities built with vision and commitment is a good start. There is a clear need for places in which to heal, places for people to live together and benefit from mutual help, and even for personal journeys to be honored, as in Jim's and Angela's cases. Nevertheless, true communities will be harder to create until economic priorities are guided by humanitarian and democratic values.

It is important for researchers to determine the costs and benefits of the types of havens described in this book and to compare them to more traditional approaches. Policy planners will need to see the economic benefits of these approaches. We clearly feel that these communities will be less expensive to maintain and yield greater health and mental benefits than more traditional treatments.

The Need for a Shift in Language

The sense of community that we find so elusive in Western society has much to do with people's ability to relate to each other and to the world around them. Allen explains how one must first be able to relate to the world before one can relate to another person. Allen also explains how one's native language plays a part in forming one's relationship with the world:

> In English, one can divide the universe into two parts: the natural and the supernatural....the supernatural is discussed as though it were apart from people, and the natural as though people were apart from it. This necessarily forces English-speaking people into a position of alienation from the world they live in. (1992, p. 60)

Allen's observations could be seen as discouraging. The English language contributes to our position of estrangement, so talking or writing about our position is only a flawed antidote, unless what we are saying is that we need to act rather than talk. In this case, our words can guide the way we live and experience our lives, and this experience can in turn change our underlying values. Reading this book is necessary to knowing what to look for, but once we have read it, the experience of true community is what we need.

Western thinking will not be changed overnight by a didactic exercise, but gradually through a conscious experiential practice, like the addicts in chapter 2 who moved out of their pathological narcissism after experiencing the collective spirit of a tight-knit Oxford House community for only a few weeks. Anybody who has suffered trauma can attest to the fact that experience can shape the psyche for the worse, but anyone who has experienced true community knows that it can reshape the psyche for the better. The deep change brought about by community life cannot be forced on anyone because it requires a will to change, some attentiveness, and a certain amount of surrendering. Once again, Oxford House residents illustrate this well in their opinion that addicts have to be ready for the experience before they can benefit from it. And even with the will to change, real community takes time.

Considering that addiction is a fundamentally self-centered process, this will to change probably has something to do with how we see ourselves in relation to others. For psychologist James Hillman (1995), "there is only one core issue for all psychology. Where is the '*me*.' Where does the 'me' begin? Where does the 'me' stop? Where does the 'other' begin?" How much we include in the boundary we draw around ourselves is indeed the defining basis of our sense of connection to anything and anyone around us. The more we are willing to consider what we have in common with others, the more we feel connected to them, and the more this sense of connection defines what we call community.

Even if you feel ready and mobilized for such a shift in your own life, we do not advocate that you try to create community by either co-opting other cultures or usurping them out of context. We humbly believe that modern American society can benefit by the lessons in this book, and that there are enough healing stories within *Havens* to illustrate a way out of disease and alienation.

Conclusion

The dramatic improvements people created in their lives through Oxford House, H.O.M.E., GROW, and other true communities are inspiring, but efforts to artificially replicate what is essentially an organic process usually meet with potential pitfalls. Many institutional interventions are still misguided efforts to reduce social ills. Solutions to addiction, old age, mental illness, and chronic medical ailments are usually sought in a piecemeal manner that fails to respect the depth and complexity of these problems, and they are therefore incapable of yielding any lasting improvements. Although helping professionals often feel good about developing these types of social interventions and are in some cases able to document some short-term gains, traditional programs fall short of the comprehensive antidotes that are needed. They fail to address the full array of interrelated symptoms that stand as obstacles to their success. More important, they fail to address the loss of a true sense of community. It seems that only the *natural* context of relationship within a community can accommodate the complexity of these problems and correct them. When this context is born out of necessity and survival, its nature is very different than when it is created for profit by a corporate entity. To try to intervene artificially, without the wholeness of true community, is to create an empty shell.

People need to recognize the difference between genuine community and institutions. Our next challenge as a nation will be to put our efforts into these types of comprehensive approaches, rather than dissipate our resources in more limited and ultimately less ecologically successful approaches. This will require that we expand our thinking to include a systems approach, and that we open ourselves to influences beyond those that have been the mainstay of the helping professions thus far.

We expected that the chapters about H.O.M.E. and GROW would be harder to write than the chapter about Oxford House, since we still needed to approach these communities, but we were surprised to find how quickly we were welcomed. What distinguished us in the eyes of these two groups was our ability to ask the right questions and to simply listen. The conversations that developed naturally with H.O.M.E. and GROW members evolved into a kind of subjective, qualitative research that nurtured the relational component of our encounters. The acceptance we found in these communities suggested that our approach had been respectful. We were spoken to without reservations. As we listened to heartbreaking stories of unimaginable suffering and healing, we noticed how candid people seemed. They were not trying to convince us of anything; they were just telling us, because we had asked. They obviously knew what they had done right, and we were won over by that. We hope you are too.

APPENDIX A

OXFORD HOUSE AND ALCOHOL AND DRUG ABUSE RESOURCES

The Oxford House Web page is a wonderful resource that describes the concept of recovery from drug and alcohol addiction. In its simplest form, an Oxford House is a democratically run, self-supporting, and drug-free home.

http://www.oxfordhouse.org/main.html

Link to the *Sixty Minutes* interview with Paul Molloy and Oxford House that occurred in 1991:

http://us.share.geocities.com/oxfordhouse_2000/OxfordHouse.rm

Link to hear the National Public Radio feature on Oxford House:

http://www.waoxfordhouse.org/media/nproh.mp3

To find an Oxford House in your state, use this directory:

http://www.oxfordhouse.org/directory.html

Oxford House Massachusetts Sober Housing Corporation:

http://www.soberhousing.com

Oxford House Hawaii state Web site:

http://www.geocities.com/oxfordhouse_2000

Oxford House Louisiana state Web site:

http://www.louisianaoxfordhouses.org

Oxford House Maryland state Web site:

http://www.marylandoxfordhouses.org

Oxford House Missouri state Web site:
   http://www.modmh.state.mo.us/ada/facts/oxford.htm

Oxford House North Carolina state Web site:
   http://www.oxfordhousenc.org

Oxford House Oregon state Web site:
   http://www.oxfordhousesoforegon.com

Oxford House Virginia state Web site:
   http://www.oxfordhouse.info/pages/1/index.htm

Oxford House Washington state Web site:
   http://www.waoxfordhouse.org

Oxford House Chapter 8 (Washington):
   http://homepages.about.com/sj97/oxfordhousesofwachapter8/

Oxford House Chapter 10 (Washington):
   http://www.waoxfdchpt10.8m.com

Oxford House Australia:
   http://home.vicnet.net.au/~emradss/addiction_recovery_centres_
   inc.htm

For questions you might have about Oxford House, you can contact:

   Fax: (301) 589-0302

   Oxford House e-mail address:

   info@oxfordhouse.org

Alcoholics Anonymous–related links:

   Online AA resources, Alcoholics Anonymous home page, index to
   the Big Book of AA Lamplighters' home page:

   http://www.recovery.org/aa/

Narcotics Anonymous–related links:

   Narcotics Anonymous, Narcotics Anonymous Online, Narcotics
   Anonymous—IRC home page:

   http://www.wsoinc.com/

Other Miscellaneous Recovery Links

The pages contained here are a collection of Internet sites put together
to give a broad base of opinions. They do not necessarily agree with
Alcoholics Anonymous and should only be taken as opinions.

Recovery-related resources, Web of Addictions, The Wall, The Lighter Side of Recovery:

http://www.dui.com/alcoholissues/Alcohol/recoveryresources.html

Other 12-step programs: Chemically Dependent Anonymous (CDA):

http://www.cdaweb.org/

The following are mailing addresses for CDA:

CDA

P.O. Box 4425

Annapolis, MD 21403

CDA: Public Information Committee

P.O. Box 864

Arnold, MD 21012

CDA: Communications, Inc.

General Services Office

P.O. Box 423

Severna Park, MD 21146-0423

For the CDA: Hot Line, call:

In Annapolis, Maryland: 1-301-260-3009

In the Washington, D.C., metro area:

(301) 369-6556

A comprehensive list of substance abuse authorities in the 50 states:

http://www.geocities.com/Substance_Abuse_Authorities.html?1026244971899

The National Council on Alcoholism and Drug Dependence fights the stigma of alcoholism and drug abuse:

http://www.ncadd.org/

The Alcohol Policy Project advocates for the prevention of alcohol problems:

http://www.cspinet.org/booze/

Join Together is an online organization taking action against substance abuse and gun violence:

http://www.jointogether.org/home/

Mothers against Drunk Driving is an advocacy organization that has been making a difference for over 20 years:
    http://www.madd.org/home/

The National Clearinghouse for Drug and Alcohol Information:
    http://www.health.org/

Physician Leadership on National Drug Policy: 37 distinguished physicians from virtually every medical specialty. They are leaders at academic and medical research institutions, hospitals, medical centers, and national professional societies across the United States:
    http://center.butler.brown.edu/plndp/

ELDERLY RESOURCES

H.O.M.E. Web site:

> Housing Opportunities and Maintenance for the Elderly
> 5414B West Roosevelt Road
> Chicago, IL 60644-1483
> Telephone: (773) 921-3200
> Fax: (773) 921-1332
> http://www.homeseniors.org/Main.asp

The Gray Panthers is a national organization of intergenerational activists dedicated to social change:

> 733 15th Street, NW
> Suite 437
> Washington, DC 20005
> Telephone: (800) 280-5362 or (202) 737-6637
> Fax: (202) 737-1160
> E-mail: info@graypanthers.org
> http://www.graypanthers.org/

The Greenhouse Project
A new model for long-term care, Green Houses are group homes that use a social and rehabilitative model of care and are designed to feel like home:

Project director: Judith Rabig

E-mail: greenhouseproject@citlink.net

http://thegreenhouseproject.com

Self-Help for the Elderly, a multiservice organization providing programs along a wellness continuum ranging from employment/training to social activities:

San Francisco Main Office

407 Sansome Street

San Francisco, CA 94111-3122

Telephone: (415) 982-9171

http://www.selfhelpelderly.org/

Little Brothers—Friends of the Elderly is a national nonprofit organization committed to relieving isolation and loneliness among the elderly:

National Headquarters

954 W. Washington Blvd., 5th Flr.

Chicago, IL 60607

Telephone: (312) 829-3055

Fax: (312) 829-3077

E-mail: national@littlebrothers.org

http://www.littlebrothers.org

Dealing with abuse toward the elderly:
http://www.crha-health.ab.ca/hlthconn/items/elder-ab.htm

Centers for Disease Control and Prevention, injuries among the elderly:
http://www.cdc.gov/health/elderly.htm

Untie the Elderly is an educational and training program for providers of long-term care to the elderly. The program is dedicated to the elimination of the use of physical and chemical restraints in nursing facilities:

The Kendal Corporation

P.O. Box 100

Kennett Square, PA 19348-0100

Telephone: (610) 388-5580

http://www.ute.kendal.org/

Elderly Accommodation Counsel is a national charity, founded in 1985, offering advice and information about all forms of accommodation for older people:

EAC, 3rd Floor

89 Albert Embankment

London SE1 7PT

Telephone: 0207820 1343

Fax: 020 7820 3970

http://www.housingcare.org/

The Council for Jewish Elderly has at its core a deep and abiding commitment to Jewish communal values and the dignity of the older person through dedication to quality programs and services for all older people and their families:

Council for Jewish Elderly

3003 W. Touhy

Chicago, IL 60645

Telephone: (773) 508-1000

http://www.cje.net/

Nutrition newsletter for the elderly:

http://www.nutritionnewsfocus.com/archive/a1/NuFrEldrly.html

Assessment of medication use in the elderly:

http://cpmcnet.columbia.edu/dept/dental/Dental_Educational_
Software/Gerontology_and_Geriatric_Dentistry/Pharmacy/
assessment_of_medication.html

Volunteers of America Elderly Services promote health and independence for seniors and provide them with opportunities to serve as community resources:

National Office

1660 Duke St.

Alexandria, VA 22314

Toll Free: (800) 899-0089

http://www.volunteersofamerica.org/xq/CFM/folder_id.118/qx/
tier2_ka.cfm

Appendix C

Mental Health Resources

The National Self-Help Clearinghouse is a not-for-profit organization that was founded in 1976 to facilitate access to self-help groups
and increase the awareness of the importance of mutual support. The
clearinghouse provides a number of services:

> http://www.selfhelpweb.org/

Schizophrenics Anonymous adds the element of self-help group support to the recovery process of people suffering from schizophrenia:

> 403 Seymour Avenue
>
> Suite 202
>
> Lansing, MI 48933
>
> Telephone: (517) 485-7168
>
> (800) 482-9534 (consumer line)
>
> http://www.sanonymous.org/

NAMI is the largest U.S. organization dedicated to improving the
lives of persons affected by serious mental illness:

> Colonial Place Three
>
> 2107 Wilson Blvd.
>
> Suite 300
>
> Arlington, VA 22201
>
> Telephone: (703) 524-7600
>
> http://www.nami.org/

Assertive Community Treatment Association involves a team treatment approach designed to provide comprehensive, community-based psychiatric treatment, rehabilitation, and support to persons with serious and persistent mental illness such as schizophrenia:

> The ACT Association
>
> Suite 102
>
> 810 E. Grand River Ave.
>
> Brighton, MI 48116
>
> Telephone: (810) 227-1859
>
> Fax: (810) 227-5785
>
> E-mail: acta@actassociation.org
>
> http://www.actassociation.org/

The Center for Mental Health Services is a component of the Substance Abuse and Mental Health Services Administration:
> http://www.mentalhealth.org/

This site offers information from NIMH about the symptoms, diagnosis, and treatment of mental illnesses:
> http://www.nimh.nih.gov/publicat/index.cfm

The Global Alliance of Mental Illness Advocacy Networks is a nonpolitical and nonsectarian network of organizations and individuals concerned about mental health. Acting as a community, the members of GAMIAN are committed to the empowerment of consumers to seek appropriate professional health care treatment for mental illness without fear of social stigma:
> http://www.gamian.org/

Mental health, self-help, and psychology information and resources:
> http://www.mental-health-matters.com/

CFS, Fibromyalgia, and MCS Resources

CFS

American Association for Chronic Fatigue Syndrome is the scientific organization that sponsors research and patient conferences on CFS:
http://www.aacfs.org/

The CFIDS Association of American is a national self-help patient advocacy organization in the United States:
http://www.cfids.org

The National CFIDS Foundation, Inc., is a national self-help patient advocacy organization in the United States:
http://www.ncf-net.org

Housing for people with multiple chemical sensitivities:
http://www.ciin.org/housing.htm

The Centers for Disease Control Web page on CFS:
http://www.cdc.gov/ncidod/diseases/cfs/

Chicago CFS Association, a local CFS support group's Web page:
http://www.enteract.com/~choward/

For information on how to get free prescription drugs:
http://www.rxassist.org

R.E.D.D., or Rnase-L Enzyme Dysfunction Disease, is based on research by Robert Suhadolnik. According to this theory, a low molecular weight

(LMW) 2'-5'A binding polypeptide (37kDa) is produced instead of the normal 80kDa protein. It is possible that LMW Rnase-L functions as a strong binder for the RNA that the body produces to fight viruses—and in fact it binds the RNA out of the process altogether. The result is that the essential last stage in the body's antiviral defense pathway is missing. To find out more, look at the R.E.D.D. home page:

> http://www.cfids-me.org/redd/

The CFIDS Association of America has released the first public service announcement (PSA) on CFIDS for television, featuring U.S. Surgeon General Dr. David Satcher. The PSA emphasizes that CFS is a serious, complex disorder that can affect people of all races and walks of life. Dr. Satcher validates the illness, saying that "We may not know the cause of [CFIDS], but the pain and suffering are real." To view the 30-second PSA in the WindowsMedia format:

> http://wm1.radiotalk.com/tcc/cfids_wm/cfids4.wmv

The CFS radio show:

> http://www.cfsaudio.4biz.net/cfsradio.htm

CFIDS/fibromyalgia self-help program book: CFIDS/Fibromyalgia Toolkit:

> http://www.cfidsselfhelp.org

CFIDS and fibromyalgia health resource:

> http://www.healthresource.com

Chronic Immunological and Neurological Diseases Association (CINDA):

> http://www.cinda.org

Frequently asked questions on Social Security disability:

> http://www.nosscr.org

Frank Albrecht's Web site, for parents of sick and worn-out kids:

> http://home.bluecrab.org/~health/sickids.html

Web site for CFIDS and fibromyalgia health resource, a good source of health information and high-quality vitamins and supplements:

> http://www.immunesupport.com

Fibromyalgia Web Sites

F.A.C.E.S., Inc., Fibromyalgia Association Created for Education and Self-Help, a network of self-help groups in the Chicago metropolitan area:

E-mail: fibrocop@hotmail.com

Telephone: Sabrina Johnson at (773) 731-1228

Fibromyalgia Network, a national support organization for individuals with FM that publishes an informative newsletter:
http://www.fmnetnews.com

Fibromyalgia Network News:
http://www.FMNetNews.com

The National Fibromyalgia Awareness Campaign:
http://fmaware.org

The Oregon Fibromyalgia Foundation:
http://www.Myalgia.com

The CF Alliance is a free, international pen-pal program for chronic fatigue syndrome, myalgic encephalomyelitis, and fibromyalgia sufferers of all ages, as well as their families and caregivers:
http://groups.yahoo.com/group/CFAlliance

Multiple Chemical Sensitivities

Multiple Chemical Sensitivity Referral and Resources, Inc., provides outreach, resources for health care professionals, patient support, and public advocacy:

508 Westgate Road

Baltimore, MD 21229-2343

Telephone: (410) 362-6400

Fax: (410) 362-6401

E-mail: donnaya@rtk.net

EI/MCS Support publishes *Canary News*, an informative newsletter dedicated to MCS issues:

1404 Judson Ave.

Evanston, IL 60201

Telephone: (847) 866-9630

The following companies offer catalogs and sell a variety of environmentally safe products for individuals with multiple chemical sensitivities and other allergic conditions, including nontoxic cleaning supplies, clothing, household paint, and air filters:

National Ecological and Environmental Delivery System
(N.E.E.D.S.)
527 Charles Avenue, 12-A
Syracuse, NY 13209
Telephone: (800) 634-1380
Fax: (800) 295-6333

Allergy Control Products, Inc.
96 Danbury Road
Ridgefield, CT 06877
Telephone: (800) 422-3878
Fax: (203) 431-8963

Other Resources for Individuals with CFS, FM, and MCS

Information about the Americans with Disabilities Act can be found at:

U.S. Department of Justice
Civil Rights Division
Public Access Section
P.O. Box 65860
Washington, DC 20277-1806
Telephone: (800) 232-9675

National Information Center for Children and Youth with
Disabilities:

P.O. Box 1492
Washington, D.C. 20013
Telephone: (202) 884-8200

Food stamps:
Telephone: (800) 252-8635

Handicapped parking placard:
Telephone: (800) 252-8980

Social Security Administration:
Telephone: (800) 772-1213

Social Security Disability Hotline:
Telephone: (800) 637-8856

Frequently asked questions on Social Security disability:
http://www.nosscr.org

Miscellaneous
Resources and Links

Simple Living Magazine provides information to help people live more simply:
   http://www.simpleliving.com/

The Simple Living Network Tools has examples and contacts for simple and healthy living:
   http://www.simpleliving.net/

Voluntary simplicity Web sites for those interested in simplifying their lives: multiple sites for finding valuable information on the simplicity movement:
   http://world.std.com/~habib/thegarden/simplicity/

The Web page of Leonard A. Jason:
   http://condor.depaul.edu/~ljason/

The Intentional Community Web site is an inclusive site for eco-villages, cohousing, residential land trusts, communes, student co-ops, urban housing cooperatives, and other related projects and dreams:
   http://www.ic.org/

The sustainable communities network Web site attempts to link citizens to resources in order to create healthy, vital, sustainable communities:
   http://www.sustainable.org/

The Bruderhof is an international movement of communal settlements dedicated to nonviolence, simplicity, and service. Currently, there are Bruderhof communities in the United States, United Kingdom, Australia, and Germany:
   http://www.bruderhof.com/us/index.htm

Communities Magazine:
   http://fic.ic.org/cmag/

Communities Online aims to address issues of sustainability, regeneration, social inclusion, and healthier economies by focusing on the use of new communications technologies in communities and neighborhoods:
   http://www.communities.org.uk/

The Society for Community Research and Action (SCRA), Division 27 of the American Psychological Association, serves many different disciplines that focus on community research and action. Our members have found that, regardless of the professional work they do, the knowledge and professional relationships they gain in the SCRA have been invaluable and invigorating. Membership provides new ideas and strategies for research and action that benefit people and improve institutions and communities. The Society for Community Research and Action was founded on the idea that social systems and environmental influences are important foci for enhancing wellness via preventive research and interventions:
   http://www.apa.org/divisions/div27/

Web site of the American Psychological Association:
   http://www.apa.org/

Web site of the American Psychological Society:
   http://www.psychologicalscience.org/

Perceived Sense of
Community Scale

To assess the sense of community experiences of individuals in Oxford Houses, we have developed a scale to measure the sense of community. It is called the Perceived Sense of Community scale (see Bishop, Chertok, & Jason, 1997). This 30-item, 5-point inventory consists of three subscales associated with community experiences: *mission* (12 items; e.g., "There is a clear sense of mission in this group"), assessing the perception that a group has goals that transcend the goals of its individual members; *reciprocal responsibility* (12 items; "Members know they can get help from the group if they need it"), assessing the perception that members both serve as resources for the group and receive responses to their individual needs; and, *disharmony* (6 items; "In this group there is the feeling that people should not get too friendly"), examining negative associations to the group. Reliability assessments of this inventory indicate that it has good internal consistency and acceptable stability. In addition, it has appropriate construct validity as a new scale for use with recovering alcoholics (Bishop, Chertok, & Jason, 1997; Bishop, Jason, Ferrari, & Cheng-Fang, 1998) and other groups (Ferrari, Jason, Olson, Davis, & Alvarez, 2002).

Please answer the following questions by indicating the extent of your agreement using the following scale:

1 = Not At All True

2 = Somewhat True

3 = Pretty Much True

4 = Very Much True

5 = Completely True

_____   1. There is a clear sense of mission in this group.

_____   2. Members know they can get help from the group if they need it.

_____   3. In this group there is the feeling that people should not get too friendly.

_____   4. The goals of this group are meaningful to members.

_____   5. People can depend on each other in this group.

_____   6. Members do not feel comfortable asking for assistance from the group.

_____   7. There is a sense of common purpose in this group.

_____   8. There is a feeling that the group looks out for its members.

_____   9. Members do not really know what the group's goals are.

_____ 10. The goals of this group are important to members.

_____ 11. The group makes you feel good for helping.

_____ 12. The atmosphere is somewhat impersonal.

_____ 13. The goals of this group are challenging.

_____ 14. Members are willing to help each other.

_____ 15. There are definite "in" and "out" groups within this group.

_____ 16. Members put a lot of effort into what they do for this group.

_____ 17. A feeling of fellowship exists between members.

_____ 18. Some people feel like outsiders at meetings.

_____ 19. You know when you are a member of this group.

_____ 20. The work done by members is appreciated.

_____ 21. Members feel like they belong to this group.

_____ 22. The atmosphere at meetings is relaxed and friendly.

_____ 23. The group makes use of everyone's skills and abilities.

_____ 24. When something needs to be done, the whole group gets behind it.

_____ 25. The goals of this group are meaningful to the larger community.

_____ 26. Members share control over what happens in this group.

_____ 27. Members of this group share common values.

_____ 28. Being a member of this group is like being part of a group of friends.

_____ 29. Members are often asked to take more responsibility.

_____ 30. There is a sense of camaraderie among members.

Scoring

Reverse score items 3, 6, 9, 12, 15, and 18. Reverse scoring is achieved by subtracting the original score from three and adding three to this difference.

There are three factor scores. Each score is the mean (add the items for that factor and divide by the number of items). For the Mission score, add the following items: 1, 4, 7, 10, 13, 16, 19, 21, 23, 25, 27, and 29. For the Reciprocal Responsibility score, add items 2, 5, 8, 11, 14, 17, 20, 22, 24, 26, 28, and 30. For the Disharmony score, add items 3, 6, 9, 12, 15, and 18.

Participatory Action Research with Chronic Fatigue Syndrome

By the early 1990s, a consensus had emerged that CFS was a relatively rare disorder (Friedberg & Jason, 1998). The demographic profiles of the patients were white, middle-class women. Initial estimates of the prevalence of this illness was 2 to 7.3 persons per 100,000 (Gunn, Connell, & Randall, 1993). This and other prevalence estimates were derived from studies in which physicians identified patients who had unexplained fatigue-related symptoms, and then referred those patients for a medical examination to determine whether they met criteria for CFS. If these estimates were correct, that would have indicated that there were fewer than 20,000 individuals with CFS in the United States.

There are several problems with epidemiological approaches that rely on physician referrals. For example, medical sociological studies have indicated that many low-income individuals do not have access to the health care system. Consequently, it would be inappropriate to estimate prevalence rates solely from treatment facilities that represent a biased sample of the population. In addition, the negative stigma of some illnesses possibly inhibits some afflicted individuals from seeking help. Of most importance, if some physicians do not believe an illness exists, as is the case with chronic fatigue syndrome, these physicians will not make referrals to epidemiological studies, and consequently this will result in an underestimate of the prevalence rates.

The low CFS prevalence numbers contrasted sharply with other sources of data from patients. For example, the high rates of telephone calls to the CDC seeking information about this illness, up to 3,000 per month, suggested that this disorder might have been more common than had been reported (McCluskey, 1993, p. 288). Patients with this syndrome were skeptical of these numbers, as there were over 20,000 individuals in the United States who were members of a CFS national self-help group. When a new disease syndrome emerges, such as CFS, studies on prevalence can shape public policy, for if few individuals are affected by the syndrome, few federal and state resources might be required for research, prevention, and intervention efforts. If CFS epidemiological studies are methodologically flawed because of their reliance on physician referrals, findings that underestimate the prevalence of CFS could minimize the seriousness of this illness.

A research team assembled in Chicago included over 15 professionals from diverse areas, including epidemiology, psychiatry, medicine, immunology, sociology, biostatistics, and community psychology. Listening to patient concerns and bringing together scientists from different disciplines is a critical step in seeking a less biased understanding and more thorough investigation of complex disease entities and conditions. People with CFS were involved throughout the design and implementation of this Chicago-based epidemiology study. These individuals included medical professionals and academic researchers who themselves had been diagnosed with the illness, representatives from the local self-help organizations, and other people with CFS who were known to the researchers. Our group did pilot studies, with the help of patient organizations, to determine the most optimal method for finding patients. We ultimately found that, using a telephone interviewing strategy, the majority of people with this condition could be contacted. Using a randomly selected community sample, rather than relying on physician referrals, over 18,000 individuals were telephone interviewed, and those with signs of CFS were given a comprehensive physical exam and psychiatric interview.

The results of the prevalence study are reported in Jason et al. (1999). Results indicated that the point prevalence of CFS was estimated at 422 per 100,000. Thus, prevalence estimates indicated that this illness may affect approximately 800,000 people in the United States, a considerably higher figure than the previous estimates. Further, rates of this illness were found to be higher in the Latino and African American groups when compared to the Caucasian sample. Rates of illness were 726 per 100,000 for the Latino sample, 337 per

100,000 for the African American sample, and 318 per 100,000 for the Caucasian sample. The highest rates of CFS were found among people from middle to low socioeconomic status, with the lowest rates among professionals. People with CFS were more likely to be unemployed, receiving disability, or working part-time compared to healthy controls.

Results of the study indicated that prevalence of CFS was higher than previously estimated. Women, Latinos, middle-aged individuals, and persons of middle to lower socioeconomic status were found to be at higher risk for this illness. These findings directly contradicted the perception that upper-class Caucasian women were the primary sufferers of this illness. In addition, only 10 percent of people with CFS in this sample had actually been diagnosed by a physician prior to participation in the study, findings that highlighted the limitations of hospital and primary care–based studies in assessing prevalence of this illness. People included in hospital and primary care–based studies may have represented a highly select group of people with CFS who are not representative of all people with this disorder. Almost all existing studies of CFS have been conducted with white samples, and yet the findings above indicate that minorities are more likely to have this syndrome, and they tend to have more disabling symptoms. In other words, the samples have been mostly white and middle class, whereas most individuals with this syndrome are minorities and not diagnosed.

People with CFS were involved in all phases of the research process, including the development of the study design and methodology, implementation, data analysis, interpretation, and dissemination of the study results. For example, people with CFS were present at all research meetings to aid in the development of the research design, to assist in selection of the measures, to assist in training staff interviewers, and to engage in problem solving around difficulties encountered in the design and implementation of the research study. People with CFS helped address specific barriers that arose during the research process, such as transportation difficulties. We not only paid individuals who were identified by our screen as possibly having CFS to participate in the interviews and medical examinations, but also provided them with transportation to the medical facility and had individuals who were bicultural conduct the interviews. In this way, we were able to include individuals in our final sample who were economically impoverished and would not have had the resources to travel to our medical site for the evaluation. People with CFS assisted in the training and education of other staff members about this illness, so that the interviewers were aware of and sensitive to the needs of people with CFS.

Our research team has in the past few years begun to work on developing and evaluating rehabilitation programs for people with chronic fatigue syndrome (Jason, Kolak et al., 2001). Much of the controversy surrounding illness management for chronic fatigue syndrome centers on the uncertainty regarding an appropriate balance between rest and activity. We believe suggestions for treatment plans and illness management need to be based upon individualized assessments and tailored to each patient's situation. This strategy, which we now call the envelope theory, was suggested to us by a member of the CFS patient community. For example, patients with chronic fatigue syndrome identified as continually overexerting themselves are advised to cut back and conserve their energy resources so that long-term gains in their tolerance to activity can be made. Others who are underexerting themselves are shown how to gradually increase their levels of activity. Our work suggests that all persons with chronic fatigue syndrome should not necessarily either increase or decrease their activity levels; instead, what is needed is to assess whether the person is within his or her energy envelope or exceeding it. We now have a NIH grant to evaluate different nonpharmacological interventions for people with CFS, and our current work in the treatment arena has been strongly influenced by suggestions and advice from those individuals who have been directly affected by this illness. Currently, the needs for safe housing for patients with CFS is another area that our research team is working on in collaboration with CFS support groups. We hope in the near future to open a setting similar to an Oxford House for individuals with CFS and other chronic illnesses.

When we address population issues that are not easily explained, such as chronic fatigue syndrome, we can advocate for research that avoids stigmatization potentially caused by biases and unexamined assumptions. In the chronic fatigue syndrome arena, key decisions were made within a sociopolitical context (Friedberg & Jason, 1998), and these biases led to underreporting in physician referral–based epidemiological studies. When sounder community-based sampling methodology was adopted and patient concerns were attended to, more accurate prevalence estimates and more appropriate demographic characteristics of patient groups were determined. These types of data, informed by an ecological analysis, can be used to guide the development of more appropriate heath care services.

These community psychology principles could be used by professionals who join in long-term collaborative relationships with persons and settings. By involving participants actively in the planning of interventions, the recipients of the programs receive support, learn to identify resources, and become better problem-solvers who are more likely to manage future problems and issues. Interventions that have been generated from collaboratively defined, produced, and implemented change efforts are more apt to endure. By involving participants in the design of the research, investigators may gain a greater appreciation of the culture and unique needs of the community, and this may increase the possibility of the research findings being used to benefit the community. This approach would analyze community traditions for responding to community problems, help evaluate or create settings that provide individuals with opportunities to continue receiving support after termination of formal treatment programs, work closely with community leaders in all aspects of the health care intervention, and assess positive and negative second-order ripple effects of an intervention.

BIBLIOGRAPHY

Adelman, M. B., & Frey, L. R. (1994). The pilgrim must embark: Creating and sustaining community in a residential facility for people with AIDS. In L. R. Frey (Ed.), *Group communication in context: Studies of natural groups* (pp. 3–22). Hillsdale, NJ: Lawrence Erlbaum Associates.

Ahrentzen, S. (2003). Double indemnity of double delight? The health consequences of shared housing and "doubling up." *Journal of Social Issues, 59,* 547–568.

Allen, P. G. (1992, originally published in 1986). *The sacred hoop: Recovering the feminine in American Indian traditions.* Boston: Beacon Press.

Anderson, J. (1999). Seniors breathe life into Chicago's past. *Chicago Tribune,* sec, 2, p. 1.

Bartel, N. R., & Guskin, S. L. (1971). A handicap as a social phenomena. In W. M. Cruickshank (Ed.), *Psychology of exceptional children* (pp. 75–114). Englewood Cliffs, NJ: Prentice Hall.

Bellah, R. N., Madsen, R., Sullivan, W. M., Swidler, A., & Tipton, S. M. (1985). *Habits of the heart. Individualism and commitment in American life.* New York: Harper & Row.

Bishop, P. D., Chertok, L., & Jason, L. A. (1997). Measuring sense of community: Beyond local boundaries. *Journal of Primary Prevention, 18,* 193–212.

Bishop, P. D., Jason, L. A., Ferrari, J. R., & Cheng-Fang, H. (1998). A survival analysis of communal-living, self-help, addiction recovery participants. *American Journal of Community Psychology 26,* 803–821.

Bogat, G. A., & Jason, L. A. (2000). Towards an integration of behaviorism and community psychology: Dogs bark at those they do not recognize. In

J. Rappaport & E. Seidman (Eds.), *Handbook of community psychology* (pp. 101–114). New York: Plenum Press.

Bond, G. R., McDonel, E. C., & Miller, L. D. (1991). Assertive community treatment and reference groups: An evaluation of their effectiveness for young adults with serious mental illness and substance abuse problems. *Psychosocial Rehabilitation Journal, 15,* 31–43.

Burgoyne, N. S., & Jason, L. A. (1991). Incorporating the ecological paradigm into behavioral preventive interventions. In P. M. Martin (Ed.), *Handbook of behavior therapy and psychological science: An integrative approach* (pp. 457–472). New York: Pergamon.

Campbell, J. (1949). *Hero of a thousand faces.* New York: Pantheon.

Centers for Disease Control and Prevention. (2000). *About chronic disease.* http://www.cdc.gov/nccdphp/about.htm.

Chesler, M. (1991). Participatory action research with self-help groups: An alternative paradigm for inquiry and action. *American Journal of Community Psychology, 19,* 757–768.

Dalton, J. H., Elias, M. J., & Wandersman, A. (2001). *Community psychology: Linking individuals and communities.* Stamford, CT: Wadsworth.

Davis, M., Jason, L. A., Ferrari, J. R., Olson, B. D., & Alvarez, J. (2004). The Oxford House project: Lessons learned from a university-community collaboration.

Duff, K. (1993). *The alchemy of illness.* New York: Pantheon.

Duffy, K. G., & Wong, F. Y. (2000). *Community psychology.* Boston: Allyn and Bacon.

Dunne, J. (1986). Sense of community in l'Arche and in the writings of Jean Vanier. *Journal of Community Psychology, 14,* 41–54.

Elgin, D. (1981). *Voluntary simplicity.* New York: Morrow.

Erikson, E. H. (1959). Identity and the life cycle: Selected papers. *Psychological Issues, 1,* 50–100.

Essock, S. M., Frisman, L. K., & Kontos, N. J. (1998). Cost-effectiveness of Assertive Community Treatment teams. *American Journal of Orthopsychiatry, 68,* 179–190.

Etzioni, A. (1993). *The spirit of community.* New York: Crown.

Fairweather, G. W. (1979). Experimental development and dissemination of an alternative to psychiatric hospitalization: Scientific methods for social change. In R. F. Munzo, L. R. Snowden, & J. G. Kelly (Eds.), *Social and psychological research in community settings* (pp. 305–342). San Francisco: Jossey-Bass.

Fellowship for Intentional Community. (1990). *Intentional communities: A guide to cooperative living.* Evansville, IN: Author.

Ferrari, J. R., Billows, W., & Jason, L. A. (1997). Matching the needs of the homeless with those of the disabled: Empowerment through caregiving. *Journal of Prevention and Intervention in the Community, 15,* 83–92.

Ferrari, J. R., Jason, L. A., Olson, B. D., Davis, M. I., & Alvarez, J. (2002). Sense of community among Oxford House residents recovering from substance abuse: Making a house a home. In A. Fischer (Ed.), *Psychological sense of community* (pp. 109–122). New York: Kluger/Plenum.

Friedberg, F., & Jason, L. A. (1998). *Understanding chronic fatigue syndrome: An empirical guide to assessment and treatment*. Washington, DC: American Psychological Association.

Goffman, E. (1961). *Asylums: Essays on the social situation of mental patients and other inmates*. Garden City, NY: Doubleday Anchor.

GROW International. (1998). The Program of Growth to Maturity [pamphlet]. A.C.T., Australia: Author.

Gunn, W. J., Connell, D. B., & Randall, B. (1993). Epidemiology of chronic fatigue syndrome: The Centers-for-Disease-Control study. In B. R. Bock & J. Whelan (Eds.), *Chronic fatigue syndrome* (pp. 83–101). New York: John Wiley & Sons.

Guthrie, D. (1999, January 29). Off the map; There's precious little left of John Baker's South Side. *Reader*, sec. 1, p. 1.

Harper, M. S. (1995). Mental health and mental health services. In P. K. H. Kim (Ed.), *Services to the aging and aged. Public polices and programs*. New York: Garland.

Hazel, K. L., & Mohatt, G. V. (2001). Cultural and spiritual pathways to sobriety: Informing substance abuse prevention and intervention for Alaska Native communities. *Journal of Community Psychology, 29*, 541–562.

Hillman, J. (1995). A psyche the size of the Earth: A psychological foreword. In T. Roszak, M. Gomes, & A. Kanner (Eds.), *Ecopsychology: Restoring the Earth, healing the mind*. San Francisco: Sierra Club Books.

H.O.M.E. (1991). *H.O.M.E. brochure*. Chicago: Author.

H.O.M.E. (2000). *Annual report 2000*. Chicago: Author.

Jason, L. A. (1997). *Community building: Values for a sustainable future*. Westport, CT: Praeger.

Jason, L. A., Davis, M. I., Ferrari, J. R., & Bishop, P. D. (2001). Oxford House: A review of research and implications for substance abuse recovery and community research. *Journal of Drug Education, 31*, 1–27.

Jason, L. A., & Glenwick, D. S. (Eds.). (2002). *Innovative strategies for promoting health and mental health across the lifespan*. New York: Springer Publishing.

Jason, L. A., Ferrari, J. R., Smith, B., Marsh, P., Dvorchak, P. A., Groessl, E. J., et al. (1997). An exploratory study of male recovering substance abusers living in a self-help, self-governed setting. *The Journal of Mental Health Administration, 24*, 332–339.

Jason, L. A., Keys, C. B., Suarez-Balcazar, Y., Taylor, R. R., Davis, M., Durlak, J., Isenberg, D. (Eds.). (2004). *Participatory community research: Theories and methods in action*. Washington, DC: American Psychological Association.

Jason, L. A., & Kobayashi, R. B. (1995). Community building: Our next frontier. *The Journal of Primary Prevention, 15*, 195–208.

Jason, L. A., Kolak, A. M., Purnell, T., Cantillon, D., Camacho, J. M., Klein, S., & Lerman, A. (2001). Collaborative ecological community interventions for people with chronic fatigue syndrome. *Journal of Prevention and Intervention in the Community, 21*, 35–51.

Jason, L. A., Olson, B. D., Ferrari, J. R., & Davis, M. I. (2003–2004). Substance abuse: The need for second-order change. *International Journal of Self Help and Self Care, 2* (2), 91–109.

Jason, L. A., Richman, J. A., Friedberg, F., Wagner, L., Taylor, R., & Jordan, K. M. (1997). Politics, science, and the emergence of a new disease: The case of chronic fatigue syndrome. *American Psychologist, 52*, 973–983.

Jason, L. A., Richman, J. A., Rademaker, A. W., Jordan, K. M., Plioplys, A. V., Taylor, R. R., McCready, W., Huang, C., & Plioplys, S. (1999). A community-based study of chronic fatigue syndrome. *Archives of Internal Medicine, 159*, 2129–2137.

Keller, E. (1985). *Reflections on gender and science.* New Haven, CT: Yale University Press.

Kelly, J. G. (1985). The concept of primary prevention: Creating new paradigms. *Journal of Primary Prevention, 5*, 269–272.

Kingry-Westergaard, C., & Kelly, J. G. (1990). A contextualist epistemology for ecological psychology. In P. Tolan, C. Keys, F. Chertok, & L. Jason (Eds.), *Researching community psychology: Issues of theory and methods* (pp. 23–31). Washington, DC: American Psychological Association.

Koebel, C. T., & Murray, M. S. (1999). Extended families and their housing in the U.S. *Housing Studies, 14*, 124–143.

Levine, M., & Perkins, D. V. (1997). *Principles of community psychology. Perspectives and applications.* New York: Oxford University Press.

Marcus, J. (2000, February 6). Gratitude for a surrogate family. *Chicago Tribune*, sec. 13, p. 2.

Marion, T. R., & Coleman, K. (1991). Recovery issues and treatment resources. In D. C. Daley & R. S. Mirium (Eds.), *Treating the chemically dependent and their families* (pp. 100–127). Newbury Park, CA: Sage Publications.

McCluskey, D. R. (1993). Pharmacological approaches to the therapy of chronic fatigue syndrome. In B. R. Bock & J. Whelan (Eds.), *Chronic fatigue syndrome* (pp. 280–297). New York: John Wiley & Sons.

McLaughlin, C., & Davidson, G. (1985). *Builders of the dawn. Community lifestyles in a changing world.* Shutesbury, MA: Sirius.

McMahon, S. D., & Pontari, B. (1993). Social support in community settings: Theory and practice. Unpublished manuscript. (Available from Susan McMahon, Department of Psychology, DePaul University, 2219 N. Kenmore Ave., Chicago, IL 60614.)

Metzner, R. (1992, June). The split between spirit and nature in European consciousness. *Science, spirituality, and the global crisis: Toward a world with a future.* Paper presented at the twelfth international transpersonal conference of the International Transpersonal Association, Prague, Czechoslovakia.

Michelson, W., & Tepperman, L. (2003). Focus on home: What time-use data can tell about caregiving to adults. *Journal of Social Issues, 59*, 591–610.

Mohatt, G., Hazel, K., Allen, J., Stachelrodt, M., Hensel, C., & Fath, R. (2001, August). *Unheard Alaska: Participatory action research on sobriety with Alaska Natives.* Paper presented at the American Psychological Association Annual Convention, San Francisco, CA.

Montgomery, H. A., Miller, W. R., & Tonigan, J. S. (1993). Differences among AA groups: Implications for research. *Journal of Studies on Alcohol, 54*, 502–504.

Morgan, A. E. (1942). *The small community.* Yellow Springs, OH: Community Service, Inc.

Muller, G. (2001). Problems of diagnostic assessment in low back patients. *Schmerz, 15*, 435–441.

Murphy, H. B. M. (1982). Culture and schizophrenia. In I. Al-Issa (Ed.), *Culture and psychopathology.* Baltimore: University Park Press.

Office of National Drug Control Policy. (2003). Drug policy information clearinghouse. http://www.whitehousedrugpolicy.gov/pdf/drug_datasum.pdf.

Ogintez, E. (1992, July 23). Program meets needs of disabled, homeless. *Chicago Tribune*, pp. 1, 2.

Oxford, J. M., & Barrett, L. (1997, September 23). Housing out of reach for many of the working poor. *St. Louis Post-Dispatch*, p. B7:2.

Purpel, D. E. (1989). *The moral and spiritual crisis in education. A curriculum for justice and compassion in education.* Granby, MA: Bergin & Garvey Publishers.

Rawls, J. (1971). *A theory of justice.* Cambridge, MA: Belknap Press of Harvard University Press.

Rudee, M., & Blease, J. (1989). *Traveler's guide to healing centers and retreats.* Santa Fe, NM: John Muir.

Sarason, S. B. (1974). *The psychological sense of community: Prospects for community psychology.* San Francisco: Jossey-Bass.

Sartre, J. P. (1956). *Being and nothingness.* London: Methuen.

Shapiro, D. (1989). Judaism as a journey of transformation. Consciousness, behavior, and society. *The Journal of Transpersonal Psychology, 21* (1), 13–59.

Siegel, B. (1990). *Love, medicine, and miracles.* New York: HarperCollins.

Smith, S. J., Easterlow, D., Munro, M., & Turner, K. M. (2003). Housing as health capital: How health trajectories and housing paths are linked. *Journal of Social Issues, 59*, 501–525.

Spretnak, C. (1991). *States of grace.* New York: HarperCollins.

Stein, M. R. (1960). *The eclipse of community.* New York: Harper Torchbook.

Tornatzky, L. G., & Fergus, E. O. (1982). Innovation and diffusion in mental health: The Community Lodge. In A. M. Jeger & R. Slotnick (Eds.),

Community mental health: A behavior-ecological perspective. New York: Plenum.

U.S. Department of Housing and Urban Development. (1998). *Rental housing assistance: The crisis continues.* Washington, DC: Author.

Watzlawick, P., Weakland, J. H., & Fisch, R. (1974). *Change: Principles of problem formation and problem resolution.* New York: W. W. Norton.

INDEX

ABOUT THE SERIES EDITOR AND ADVISORY BOARD

CHRIS E. STOUT, Psy.D., MBA, holds a joint governmental and academic appointment in Northwestern University Medical School, and serves as Illinois's first Chief of Psychological Services. He served as an NGO Special Representative to the United Nations, was appointed by the U.S. Department of Commerce as a Baldridge Examiner, and served as an advisor to the White House for both political parties. He was appointed to the World Economic Forum's Global Leaders of Tomorrow. He has published and presented more than 300 papers and 29 books. His works have been translated into six languages. He has lectured across the nation and internationally in 16 countries, visiting more than 60 nations. He has been on missions around the world and has summited three of the world's seven summits.

BRUCE E. BONECUTTER, Ph.D., is Director of Behavioral Services at the Elgin Community Mental Health Center, the Illinois Department of Human Services state hospital serving adults in greater Chicago. He is also a Clinical Assistant Professor of Psychology at the University of Illinois at Chicago. A clinical psychologist specializing in health, consulting, and forensic psychology, Dr. Bonecutter is also a longtime member of the American Psychological Association Taskforce on Children and the Family.

JOSEPH A. FLAHERTY, M.D., is Chief of Psychiatry at the University of Illinois Hospital, a Professor of Psychiatry at the University of Illinois College of Medicine, and a Professor of Community Health Science at the UIC College of Public Health. He is a Founding Member of the Society for the Study of Culture and Psychiatry. Dr. Flaherty has been a consultant to the World Health Organization, the National Institutes of Mental Health, and the Falk Institute in Jerusalem.

MICHAEL HOROWITZ, Ph.D., is President and Professor of Clinical Psychology at the Chicago School of Professional Psychology, one of the nation's leading not-for-profit graduate schools of psychology. Earlier, he served as Dean and Professor of the Arizona School of Professional Psychology. A clinical psychologist practicing independently since 1987, his work has focused on psychoanalysis, intensive individual therapy, and couples therapy. He has provided Disaster Mental Health Services to the American Red Cross. Dr. Horowitz's special interests include the study of fatherhood.

SHELDON I. MILLER, M.D., is a Professor of Psychiatry at Northwestern University and Director of the Stone Institute of Psychiatry at Northwestern Memorial Hospital. He is also Director of the American Board of Psychiatry and Neurology, Director of the American Board of Emergency Medicine, and Director of the Accreditation Council for Graduate Medical Education. Dr. Miller is also an Examiner for the American Board of Psychiatry and Neurology. He is a Founding Editor of the American Journal of Addictions, and Founding Chairman of the American Psychiatric Association's Committee on Alcoholism.

DENNIS P. MORRISON, Ph.D., is Chief Executive Officer at the Center for Behavioral Health in Indiana, the first behavioral health company ever to win the JCAHO Codman Award for excellence in the use of outcomes management to achieve health care quality improvement. He is President of the Board of Directors for the Community Healthcare Foundation in Bloomington, and he has been a member of the Board of Directors for the American College of Sports Psychology. Dr. Morrison has served as a consultant to agencies including the Ohio Department of Mental Health, Tennessee Association of Mental Health Organizations, Oklahoma Psychological Association, the

North Carolina Council of Community Mental Health Centers, and the National Center for Heath Promotion in Michigan.

WILLIAM H. REID, M.D., MPH, is a clinical and forensic psychiatrist and consultant to attorneys and courts throughout the United States. He is Clinical Professor of Psychiatry at the University of Texas Health Science Center. Dr. Reid is also an Adjunct Professor of Psychiatry at Texas A & M College of Medicine and Texas Tech University School of Medicine, as well as a Clinical Faculty member at the Austin Psychiatry Residency Program. He is Chairman of the Scientific Advisory Board and Medical Advisor to the Texas Depressive & Manic-Depressive Association, as well as an Examiner for the American Board of Psychiatry & Neurology. He has served as President of the American Academy of Psychiatry and the Law, as Chairman of the Research Section for an International Conference on the Psychiatric Aspects of Terrorism, and as Medical Director for the Texas Department of Mental Health and Mental Retardation.

About the Authors

LEONARD JASON, Ph.D., is a Professor of Psychology at DePaul University in Chicago, where he heads the Center for Community Research. He has published 384 articles and 65 chapters on preventive school-based interventions; the prevention of alcohol, tobacco, and drug abuse; media interventions; and program evaluation. His own experience with chronic fatigue syndrome has been a motivating factor in his efforts to promote the healing effects of community on chronic illness and other conditions described in *Havens: Stories of True Community Healing*. He has been on the editorial boards of seven peer-reviewed psychology journals, and he has edited or written 17 books. He has served on review committees of the National Institute of Drug Abuse and the National Institute of Mental Health, and has received more than $16 million in federal grants to support his research. He is a former President of the Division of Community Psychology of the American Psychological Association and a past Editor of *The Community Psychologist*. He has received three media awards from the American Psychological Association, and he is frequently asked to comment on policy issues for the media.

MARTIN PERDOUX, MAAT, is a writer living in Chicago and a registered art therapist with nine years of practice in psychiatry and special education. He has presented several conference papers and workshops, and his writing has been published in the Chicago *Reader*,

The Reader's Guide to Arts and Entertainment, and *Art Therapy: Journal of the American Art Therapy Association.* His memoir, partly about his own recovery from heroin addiction, is under consideration for publication. He is a Consulting Editor at Behavior OnLine (http://www.behavior.net), a leading online forum for mental health professionals. He was the recipient of several grants, residencies, and awards for his writing, including the state's highest artistic award in prose, the Illinois Arts Council Artist Fellowship Award. Recent awards include three writing residencies at the Ragdale Foundation, a 2002 Chicago Department of Cultural Affairs grant, a 2002 School of the Art Institute of Chicago Faculty Enrichment Grant and Roger Brown Residency, and a 2002 Illinois Arts Council Special Assistance Grant in literature.